the SOURDOUGH BREAD BOWL Cookbook

For Parties, Holiday Celebrations, Family Gatherings, and Everyday Meals

John Vrattos

Lisa Messinger

SQUAREONE
PUBLISHERS

COVER DESIGNER: Phaedra Mastrocola and Jacqueline Michelus
INTERIOR ART: Vicki Renoux
COVER PHOTOGRAPH: Getty Images, Inc.
EDITOR: Marie Caratozzolo • TYPESETTER: Gary A. Rosenberg

Square One Publishers
115 Herricks Road • Garden City Park, NY 11040
(877) 900-BOOK • (516) 535-2010
www.squareonepublishers.com

Library of Congress Cataloging-in-Publication Data

Vrattos, John.
  The sourdough bread bowl cookbook : for parties, holiday celebrations,
family gatherings, and everyday meals / John Vrattos, Lisa Messinger.
    p. cm.
  Includes index.
  ISBN 0-7570-0149-1 (pbk.)
1. Cookery (Sourdough) 2. Stuffed foods (Cookery) I. Messinger, Lisa,
1962– II. Title.

TX770.S66V73 2004
641.8—dc22

                                                                    2004022849

Printed in the United States of America

10 9 8 7 6 5 4 3 2 1

Contents

To Francesca, Alexia, and Joel,
who have helped our bread bowls
runneth over with love
for many years.

Acknowledgments

We greatly thank publisher Rudy Shur of Square One Publishers for his enthusiasm, support, and words of wisdom regarding this special book; and our editor, Marie Caratozzolo, for her invaluable input and editorial guidance. Warm thanks to Leo Pearlstein of Lee & Associates/Western Research Kitchens for introducing the two of us (little realizing the single force our kindred spirits would become). Thanks to Dick Willson and Norm Andrews. And much appreciation to John's colleagues at Maple Leaf Bakery.

We heartily thank the outstanding, award-winning professional chefs—Bren Boyd, Salvatore John Campagna, Mark Franz, John Kane, Ian Morrison, Bruce Paton, Steve Scarabosio, Clyde Serda, and Jay Veregge, as well as John's brother Chris Vrattos and cousin Peter Vroundgos—who you will meet on pages of this book. We would also like to acknowledge the Chefs Association of the Pacific Coast.

John wants to personally thank his wife Francesca, daughter Alexia, and mom Emily for their support and contribution. Lisa adds her personal thanks to Copley News Service and its editorial director Glenda Winders for giving her nationally syndicated cookbook review column a wonderful home for the last decade. Finally, for their loving support, she thanks her husband Joel Weiss, brother Robert Messinger, and parents Joan and Harold Messinger.

Introduction

San Francisco's world-famous Fisherman's Wharf is recognized for more than its memorable view of the Golden Gate Bridge spanning the magnificent bay. This picturesque stretch of restaurants and outdoor cafes is where the practice of serving piping hot clam chowder in crusty sourdough bread bowls began.

We have enjoyed this delectable taste treat firsthand. We have also discovered that the crisp, crunchy bowls made from hollowed-out sourdough bread rounds are perfect for holding foods other than clam chowder. How did we make this discovery? For starters, we both love bread bowls and had been experimenting with new filling ideas for years. John is a gourmet cook, and has worked in the sourdough bread business for nearly three decades. He was even on the team that created spinach dip in a bread bowl—a promotional appetizer for the 1985 Super Bowl that immediately swept the nation. As a syndicated food columnist and cookbook author, I have always appreciated and enjoyed good food and the art of creative cooking. Our common appreciation of tasteful cuisine (and love of that famous chowder served on Fisherman's Wharf) inspired us to join forces in compiling other recipes that are perfect for serving in bread bowls. *The Sourdough Bread Bowl Cookbook* is the result of our efforts.

Whether your loaf is out-of-the-oven fresh or store-bought, we begin with a chapter on bread bowl basics. In it, you'll find tips for selecting the best bread, easy-to-follow steps for turning it into a bowl, and recommendations for the best fillings. It even includes a great recipe for baking your own sourdough bread.

What follows next are over 100 sumptuous kitchen-tested recipes, proving that sourdough bread bowls are not just for chowder anymore. These hollowed-out rounds can serve as beautiful party centerpieces filled with luscious dips and mouthwatering spreads. They are also chic edible vessels for salads, appetizers, entrées, and even desserts that deliciously soak up the dressings, sauces, and other flavorful filling ingredients. You'll find traditional dishes such as Fisherman's Wharf-Style Clam Chowder, Chicken Noodle Casserole, and Warm Cobb Salad, as well as innovative creations like the appetizing Teriyaki Chicken Bowl, California Wine-and-Cheese Stew, and Warm Baja Shrimp Taco Dip.

Because we know that holidays are special, and every holiday menu can benefit from at least one scene-stealing dish, we present "Hits for the Holidays." This chapter offers bread bowl ideas for special days during the year. You can ring in the New Year with Champagne Chicken a l'Orange, celebrate Easter with a Spicy Lamb Easter Basket, and enjoy a Chili Dog Casserole on Independence Day.

Although sourdough—with its thick, sturdy crust and unobtrusive flavor—is a clear-cut winner when it comes to bread bowl cuisine, it is not the only bread type that can house foods successfully. Rounds of hearty rye, pumpernickel, and whole wheat, as well as thick-crusted rounds of Italian semolina, are other choices. We have devoted an entire chapter to delectable creations that are served in bowls other than sourdough. You'll find our Sky-High Reuben piled into a round of hearty rye, a luscious Noodle Kugel nestled in a pumpernickel, and a garlicky Italian semolina round filled with a Caesar Salad that's fit for a king!

As an added bonus, throughout the book you'll find outstanding bread bowl recipes developed by top restaurant chefs who have honed their culinary skills at such restaurants as the famous Scoma's on Fisherman's Wharf and the prestigious Tadich Grill—San Francisco's oldest eatery.

Whether you're hosting a Super Bowl party, preparing a meal for the family, or bringing something special to a potluck dinner, our easy-to-follow, fun-to-use cookbook will help you get started preparing and serving meals in this unique way. Remember, bread bowls are communal centerpieces that encourage shared eating enjoyment and warm conversation. It is our sincerest hope that you enjoy them as much as we do. ***Bowl Appetit!***

1. Creating **Your** **Bread**Bowls

Chefs at the picturesque, bustling restaurants of San Francisco's famous Fisherman's Wharf certainly made a splash when they popularized bread bowls by filling them with scrumptious piping hot clam chowder. However, they were far from the first to recognize the ease and delectability of using bread bowls. Although this is the first book devoted to the art, the concept is not a new one:

> *Take a manchet of French bread of a day old, chip it and cut a round hole in the top, save the piece whole, and take out the crumb, then make a composition of a boild or a rost Capon, minced and stampt with Almond paste . . . sweet herbs chopped fine, cinnamon, nutmeg . . . and pistaches . . . fill the Loaf, and stop the hole with the piece, and boil it in a clean cloth . . . or bake it in an oven.*

So wrote English chef Robert May in *The Accomplisht Cook.* The 1660 work—by far the most important cookbook of its time—included dishes of the Restoration era, as well as recipes that were used as far back as Medieval times. By the way, in the above quote, the "oven" referred to for baking the loaf was not an oven as we know it today. Rather, it was a simple enclosed hot-air container that had been used since the fifth century.

Now you are about to join the ranks of cooks, who, over the centuries, have learned how easy and delicious it is to use bread bowls in their cooking. In this opening chapter, we'll fill you in on everything you'll need to know to get started. First, you'll discover how to choose, store, and prepare your bread. Next you'll learn the super-simple technique for hollowing out the loaf and transforming it into a bowl. Helpful, easy-to-follow drawings are provided to ensure successful results. Although we recommend buying ready-made loaves for the bowls, some cooks may prefer making the bread from scratch. For those adventurous souls, we have provided a classic recipe for making delicious sourdough bread rounds that begins with an outstanding starter mixture.

After presenting the information on the bowls themselves, we turn our attention to the filling. You'll be amazed at the wide variety of ingredients that are excellent choices for piling into a bread bowl. You will also learn which ingredients to avoid. Easy-to-follow instructions for cooking the filling directly in the bowl itself (when applicable) are provided, as well as recommendations for serving your masterpiece. So get ready to embark on a culinary experience that is taste tempting, visually appealing, and lots of fun.

WHY SOURDOUGH?

If you have ever sampled a chowder or dip that was housed in a sourdough bowl, you will immediately understand why this type of bread is the preferred choice. Most obviously—and most important—sourdough bread has a thicker, heartier crust than most other breads. This makes it the ideal container, especially for those saucy fillings that might leak through or erode other kinds of bread that are less substantial. Additionally, sourdough's flavor is unobtrusive enough to avoid interfering with the flavor of the filling ingredients, yet distinctive enough to add pizzazz to whatever it contains. And let's not forget its marvelous crisp yet chewy texture. While maintaining its sturdy crust, the bowl itself will soak up the delicious filling, and become an edible serving piece. We have formulated the recipes in the book to complement both the flavor and texture of sourdough.

Although bowls made of sourdough bread are preferred and the primary focus of this book, they are not the only types that work for housing certain recipes. Rounds of hearty rye, pumpernickel, and whole wheat, as well as certain sweet breads can make excellent choices, too. For this reason, our final chapter includes special recipes that are the perfect fillings for a number of bread bowl varieties.

Baking sourdough bread at home is a timely, somewhat difficult process that typically is not recommended. The high-top rounds used to make the bowls require a thick crust that results from the intense heat of commercial ovens (particularly stone-brick ovens). Most home ovens do not generate this type of heat. Furthermore, the excellent quality of today's bakery and store-bought sourdough loaves makes it unnecessary to bake them from scratch. This adds to the appeal and convenience of serving food in bread bowls. Sometimes, however, it's fun to experiment at home. If you would like to try making your own loaves, we have provided a recipe beginning on page 7.

SHOPPING FOR THE RIGHT BREAD

For your convenience, the recipes in this book have been formulated to fit in bowls made from unsliced standard-sized sourdough rounds (also called *boule*) that are eight to ten inches in diameter and weigh 1 to 1¾ pounds. They are usually available in local neighborhood bakeries. Many supermarkets carry these rounds in their fresh bakery department, and also offer packaged commercial varieties in the bread section. We have found that a number of bakeries, including those in supermarkets, typically bake only a few fresh sourdough rounds each day. Most take phone orders, although the requirements for this can vary. Some places require the order to be placed days before, while others need only a few hours notice.

In addition to neighborhood supermarkets and bakeries, a number of bread companies sell their sourdough rounds (in varying sizes) over the Internet. When shopping online, be sure to specify "unsliced" rounds.

When shopping in a supermarket or bakery, where you can actually see and possibly touch the bread (if packaged), keep the following guidelines in mind for optimum selection. Begin by examining the crust, always opting for one with a thick, sturdy bottom. When shopping for most types of bread, we tend to choose the softest loaves, but this is not the case with sourdough. The overall crust should crackle a bit; it should not be overly soft. Gently squeeze the bread from top to bottom. If it is especially soft, it may be underbaked, a somewhat common baking error. Even if the crust is not crisp, don't worry. Later in this chapter, we'll show you how to "bake-off" the hollowed rounds. This simple step, which takes only a few minutes, makes the loaves even sturdier before adding the filling; however, it is still preferable to begin with the crispest crust possible.

Notice the bread's color—the darker the crust the better. The Tadich Grill, one of San Francisco's oldest, most famous restaurants, is well aware of the goodness of such bread and has its own "Tadich Loaf" made especially for its use. The dark loaf even looks burnt. A similarly baked "Scoma's Loaf" is the signature round used at the legendary Scoma's restaurant on San Francisco's Fisherman's Wharf. If you are placing an order with a bakery, you might want to request a dark loaf. Just be sure that the bread doesn't have a charcoal odor, which signifies it is actually burnt, and not desirable.

STORING YOUR BREAD ROUNDS

Ideally, of course, it's best to purchase your sourdough round on the same day you plan to use it; however, this is not always possible or convenient. If you are going to use the bread within a few days, place it in a paper bag to maintain its crisp crust. Close the bag tightly and store at room temperature (it will stale more quickly in the refrigerator). One of the benefits of unsliced bread is that it becomes stale at a slower pace than sliced varieties. If the bread is stored for a number of days or in a humid environment, the crust may soften somewhat. The bake-off process, explained later in this chapter, will help restore the desired crispness.

You can also freeze sourdough rounds for later use. Simply place them in double plastic freezer bags and store them for up to a month. To thaw, leave the bread in the unopened bags at room temperature for about two hours. Do not thaw in an oven—conventional or microwave. Once thawed, follow the bake-off procedure.

MAKING YOUR OWN SOURDOUGH ROUNDS

Ready-made sourdough rounds are outstanding (not to mention convenient) for making bread bowls, but if you'd like to try baking your own, here's a tried-and-true recipe to follow. One word of warning—although the process is easy, it does take time. You see, all sourdough breads must begin with a good *starter*—a flour and water mixture that contains the yeast needed for the bread to rise and give it flavor. Preparing a proper starter (in which you will be creating your own *wild* yeast) takes a few days. Unlike domesticated commercial yeasts used in standard yeast breads, wild sourdough yeasts can survive in a wide range of temperatures and acidic environments. They also give sourdough bread its unique tangy taste.

CREATING A STARTER

A sourdough starter is a living organism. Once made, you can use this "mother starter" over and over again, as long as you continue to feed and nurture it. To help ensure successful results, keep the following tips in mind:

- Because the starter can react to metal, the mixing bowls, storage jars, and all other kitchen utensils used in its preparation should be made of glass, ceramic, wood, or plastic.

- Use bowls that are large enough to allow the developing starter to expand.

- Use filtered water. Chlorinated water will destroy yeast organisms. If chlorinated water is the only type available, leaving it in the open air for twenty-four hours will cause the chlorine to evaporate.

The following recipe, which requires four simple steps, will yield 1¼ to 2 cups of starter (1 cup will be used to bake the bread in the following recipe; the remainder will be used to replenish the starter for future use).

Step 1

---

8 ounces organic grapes,*
or ⅛ cup apple juice or beer

⅛ cup water, at room temperature

¾ cup all-purpose white flour

---

*Organic grapes are free of pesticide residue, which can ward off the bacteria that are necessary for fermentation.

1. With your fingers, gently squeeze the grapes through a strainer to get $\frac{1}{8}$ cup juice, free of seeds, skin, or pulp. Combine the juice with the water to equal $\frac{1}{4}$ cup liquid.

2. Place the liquid in a food processor or electric mixer, add the flour, and mix for 3 to 5 minutes to form a soft dough. Transfer to a large bowl.

3. Cover the bowl with plastic wrap and place in a warm (70ºF to 75ºF) draft-free area for 24 to 48 hours, or until the starter doubles in volume.

Step 2

$\frac{3}{4}$ cup all-purpose white flour

$\frac{1}{4}$ cup water, at room temperature

1. Place the fermenting starter mixture, flour, and water in the food processor (or mixer), mix 3 to 5 minutes, and then transfer back to the bowl.

2. Again, cover the bowl with fresh plastic wrap and place in a warm draft-free area for 48 hours, or until the starter doubles in volume.

Step 3

1 cup all-purpose white flour

$\frac{1}{2}$ cup water, at room temperature

1 tablespoon salt

1. Place the fermenting starter mixture flour, water, and salt in the food processor (or mixer), mix 3 to 5 minutes, then transfer back to the bowl.

2. Cover the bowl with fresh plastic wrap and place in a warm draft-free area for 24 hours. The starter will double and perhaps triple during this time.

Step 4

1 $\frac{1}{2}$ cups all-purpose white flour

$\frac{3}{4}$ cup water, at room temperature

1 tablespoon plus 2 teaspoons salt

1. Place the fermenting starter mixture flour, water, and salt in the food processor (or mixer), mix 3 to 5 minutes, then transfer back to the bowl.

2. Cover the bowl with fresh plastic wrap and place in a warm draft-free area for

24 hours. Again, the starter will have at least doubled and perhaps tripled during this time. It is now ready to use.

MAKING THE BREAD

Now that your starter is ready, it's time to make the bread. The following recipe, which yields two 24- to 26-ounce rounds, requires 1 cup of starter. Place the unused portion in a clean bowl, cover with plastic wrap, and store in the refrigerator, where it will remain dormant. It's best to use the starter again within 72 hours. Simply remove it from the refrigerator, let it come to room temperature, and repeat Steps 2, 3, and 4.

You can bake the rounds either on baking pans or baking stones. You will also need the following ingredients:

1 cup sourdough starter

6 cups all-purpose white flour

2 tablespoons plus 1/4 teaspoon salt

2 cups water, at room temperature

1/4 cup cornmeal

Preparing the Dough

1. Place all of the ingredients except the cornmeal in a large mixing bowl or food processor. Mix for 5 to 6 minutes at low speed, and then an additional 2 to 3 minutes at high speed to form a soft dough. Transfer to a large bowl.

2. Cover the bowl with plastic wrap, and allow it to ferment at room temperature for 1 hour, or until doubled in size. Punch down the dough, then let it continue to ferment another hour or so, until it is shiny and does not spring back when pressed with your finger. Once the dough is punched, there will be minimal rising.

Shaping the Rounds

1. Divide the dough in half, and shape each half into a ball.

2. Place each ball in a bowl, dust with flour, and allow to rest at room temperature for 1 1/2 hours. Again, any rising during this time will be minimal.

Baking the Bread

1. Preheat the oven to 450ºF. If using baking sheets, double up two under each loaf to buffer the direct oven heat from

below. If using a baking stone, place it in the oven before preheating.

2. Generously dust a flat clean surface with flour. Carefully remove the round loaves from the bowls and place them flat side down (the side flattened by the bottom of the bowl) on the surface.

3. Using a sharp knife, score the top of the loaves with 1/2-inch-deep slashes in a tic-tac-toe pattern. In addition to being decorative, the slashes will help release any gases that may be in the dough.

4. Sprinkle the baking sheets with cornmeal and place the rounds on top. If possible, place both loaves on the middle rack of the oven; if not, place one on the top rack and the other on the bottom rack.

5. After the loaves have been baking 20 minutes, turn the pans. Also, using a misting bottle, spray the sides of the oven once or twice to create steam. (Be careful not to mist the loaves or baking sheet). Shut the oven door immediately to trap the steam, which will help form the bread's crackly, shiny crust.

6. Continue to bake another 25 to 40 minutes, or until the loaves are golden brown. Remove from the oven and place on racks. When cool enough to handle, tap the bottoms. If it sounds hollow, the bread is done. If not, return the bread to the oven and bake some more.

7. Allow the loaves to cool completely—about 1 hour. The bread will continue to bake as it cools.

There you have it! Your beautiful sourdough rounds are now ready. You can eat them as is, or turn them into bread bowls to serve with any of the delicious fillings presented in the following chapters. Making your own bread *does* require a little time, but the process itself is not a difficult one. And once you have tasted the delectable results, you'll know the effort was worth it.

PREPARING THE BREAD BOWL

Preparing your sourdough bread bowl is simple. It involves baking-off the round, allowing it to cool, and then hollowing-out the inner bread.

Baking-Off the Round

Baking-off a fresh round, whether store bought or homemade, makes its firm bottom and crust even sturdier. Begin by preheating the oven to 425°F. Place the bread (without slits or cuts) in the center of the oven for about seven minutes. It may get darker during this time, which is preferable; but allow it to darken only slightly. The high oven temperature ensures that the bread inside the loaf will stay soft; baking at a low temperature will steal the bread's moisture, causing it to dry out. After the bake-off, place the round on a rack and set it on the counter, where it will continue to bake until it cools—about thirty minutes.

If you are making a bowl from bread that is not freshly baked, but rather one that has been stored for a few days or just thawed from the freezer, make a few slits in the top before placing it in the oven. Also sprinkle or spritz it with a little water (a spray bottle works great). If you have bought a par-baked round—one that is only partially baked—follow the baker's instructions for finishing the process. If none have been provided, preheat the oven to 450°F and bake the loaf for twelve to fifteen minutes, or until the crust is brown and crisp. Remove the loaf before it gets too dark, and let it continue to bake on the counter as it cools.

Although baking-off the bread isn't a necessary step, it is suggested. More than likely, any fully baked sourdough round you buy will be good enough to hollow out as it is and fill. The bowl is not likely to leak or get soggy, and the crispness of the crust should be acceptable. So if you are pressed for time, you can skip the baking-off step and simply hollow out the bread. This is particularly acceptable for recipes such as thick dips and lightly dressed salads, which do not contain much liquid. Whenever possible, however, we recommend taking the few minutes necessary to bake-off your sourdough round—just like the pros do.

Hollowing Out the Bread Bowl

After you have baked-off your wonderfully crisp sourdough round and it has cooled, it's time to form the bowl. This brief, simple hollowing-out process is explained in the steps below, along with easy-to-follow drawings to ensure optimal results.

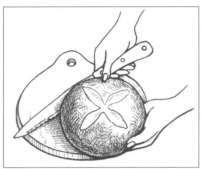

1. Begin with a sourdough round and a large serrated knife.

2. Make a straight cut across the dome of the round, about 1 to 1 1/2 inches from the top.

3. Remove the top, which can be used as a lid or cut into strips and enjoyed with the meal.

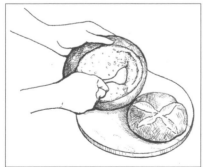

4. Using a tablespoon, gently pull the inner bread from the round, leaving a 3/4- to 1-inch thickness along the sides.

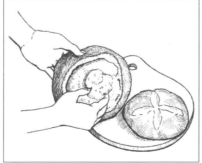

5. Grab the bread with your hand. With a twisting motion, remove it in one piece.

6. The bowl is now ready to fill with any and all of the wonderful recipes that follow.

Some of our recipes utilize the bread that has been removed from the bowl. However, when the recipe doesn't call for the bread, you can still use it to make homemade breadcrumbs or croutons. For breadcrumbs, simply break the bread into chunks, place them on an unoiled baking sheet, and bake at 350°F for twenty-five to thirty-five minutes or until dry. Once the bread cools, crumble it further and store an airtight container. For croutons, cut the bread into cubes, place them on an unoiled baking sheet, and bake at 325°F for thirty to forty minutes until toasted, but not burned. Once cooled, store the croutons in an airtight container. If desired, you can season the breadcrumbs and/or croutons with salt, pepper, garlic powder, onion powder, or other favorite spices and herbs.

COOKING AND SERVING TIPS

After the easy process of hollowing out your bread bowl, it's ready to go . . . and here's your chance to really get creative. As you will soon see, filling choices are no longer limited to the traditional dips and chowders made famous on Fisherman's Wharf. From appetizing spreads and salads to hearty casseroles and stews to taste-tempting desserts, the choices for spooning into a bread bowl are nearly limitless.

The majority of recipes in our book require basic ingredients and simple preparation methods. Mouthwatering and visually appealing, they have all been kitchen tested for successful results. We encourage you to use them as springboards for formulating creative fillings of your own. There are, however, some simple guidelines regarding ingredient choices, cooking methods, and serving ideas that you should keep in mind for best results.

Choosing the Right Ingredients

Although a wide range of ingredients work well when housed in a crisp, hearty bread bowl, some make better choices than others—and a few should be used sparingly or avoided altogether. Keep the following general rules in mind for successful fillings every time:

❑ **Don't overdo the liquid.** All of the recipes in this book have passed the "kitchen counter" test to ensure that they contain the right amount of liquid. We filled the bowls, and then let them sit on the kitchen counter for many hours (much longer than they would sit on a dinner table or as part of a buffet spread). If you decide to stretch your creative talents and alter the recipes in this book or choose to fill your bread bowl with a recipe from your personal files, just be careful not to use too much liquid. Be conservative or you may find your bread bowl getting soggy or leaking. Thin broths and runny sauces, for instance, are not good choices. Thicker, chowder-like soups and stews, however, will work.

❑ **Consider size and texture.** Dishes that include bite-sized ingredients, such as potato and carrot chunks, pearl onions, beef stew meat, and diced ham, chicken, and turkey work beautifully as bread bowl fillers. These foods tend to hold up well and present a satisfying "meal-in-a-bowl" result. Ingredients with interesting textures, such as nuts, kidney beans, chickpeas, and other legumes are also good choices as they add both taste and visual appeal. Other suggested foods that offer the right size and texture include (but are not limited to):

- Cooked sliced sausage and frankfurters.
- Cooked and drained ground meats, such as beef, turkey, chicken, and lamb.
- Cooked crabmeat, scallops, and shrimp.
- Nuts such as cashews, walnuts, pecans, and pistachios.
- Beans and legumes, such as lentils, black beans, white beans, green peas, lima beans, and navy beans.
- Corn kernels, broccoli florets, sliced mushrooms, and cut or sliced onions.

❑ **Choose creamy, smooth ingredients.** Rich, creamy ingredients that blend well, such as sour cream, cream cheese, peanut butter, butter, and gravies, are good choices. Just about any type of cheese—both hard (grated), semi-soft, and soft varieties that melt well are also outstanding. Chocolate chunks, chips, and syrup, as well as jams and jellies are often used for dessert fillings.

❑ **Select ingredients that layer well.** Many fillings that are baked right in the bowl are layered for the best results. This is especially true for those recipes in which the bowl is cut into wedges and served. Ingredients that work well to form flat layers include sliced meats, such as ham, beef, chicken, and turkey. Slices of hard and semi-soft cheeses also work well, as do vegetables like zucchini and eggplant rounds. And don't forget about tortillas and slices of hearty sourdough bread.

❑ **Avoid starchy ingredients.** The bread bowls themselves are a starch, so we don't recommend filling them with pasta, rice, or potatoes. You can include these foods in a soup or casserole, but we don't suggest them as the sole ingredient.

❑ **Use spreads when appropriate.** When the opportunity arises, consider lining the interior of the bread bowl with an appropriately flavored spread before adding the filling. For Mediterranean-style soups or stews, for instance, you can first spread some flavorful garlicky basil pesto inside the bowl. If it's an Indian-inspired dip or spread you will be adding, serve it in a bowl that is lined with a sweet preserve or spicy chutney. The right spread will add a spark of flavor and a complementary dimension to a wide variety of dishes.

Cooking in Your Bread Bowl

Although most of our fillings are prepared before they are added to the bowls, in some recipes they are baked right in them. Not only is this convenient, it allows an even greater melding of ingredients with the sourdough bread that houses it.

Although baking times will vary somewhat, the basic procedure is the same (and really quite simple). Unless otherwise specified, after filling the bowl, wrap it in aluminum foil, leaving the lid off and the top uncovered, and place in the center of a preheated 350°F oven. If the ingredients are already cooked, and the filling is just being warmed, bake the bowl for about fifteen minutes. If the filling needs to be cooked, baking time will depend on the specific recipe instructions—usually between thirty and fifty minutes. In either case, carefully remove the foil for its last three minutes in the oven to give the bread some extra crunch.

If the filling has already been prepared, you can heat the empty bread bowl by placing it unwrapped in a preheated 350°F oven for three to five minutes. Once warm, remove it from the oven, add the prepared filling, and serve.

Serving From Your Bread Bowl

Your bread bowl is the ultimate serving piece. After all, you get to eat this delicious dish along with your meal! Depending on the contents of the bowl, there are a number of ways to enjoy serving it:

❑ Ladle or spoon servings from the bowl, and then rip off pieces of the flavorful bread to enjoy with the meal. Of course, if the filling is a creamy dip or a savory soup or stew, you can also dip the bread back into the bowl before eating it.

❑ Create an "open-faced sandwich" by ripping off pieces of the bowl, placing them on your plate, and topping with the filling.

❑ For layered dishes or casseroles, you can cut the entire bowl into pie-shaped wedges before serving.

❑ After enjoying the contents of the bowl, you can eat the flavorful bread as a separate, delectable course.

One thing is certain. There is no right or wrong way to serve or eat your delicious bread bowl and its mouthwatering contents.

TIME TO GET STARTED

Now that you are armed and ready, it's time for the bread bowl creations to begin. Keep in mind that by following the recipes in the following chapters exactly as written, you should achieve successful results each time. However, we also encourage you to experiment and create dishes of your own. Just follow the helpful guidelines presented in this chapter. Ready? Let's get started!

2.Hits**for**the Holidays

Whether it is for Thanksgiving, Christmas, or the Fourth of July, every holiday menu can benefit from at least one memorable, scene-stealing dish. And nothing fills the bill better than a special bread bowl presentation. It doesn't matter if this unique serving piece houses a soup, entrée, or condiment, it will always draw attention and admiration, as well as lively conversation. Furthermore, as you will see, when filled with the right foods, a bread bowl provides more than just eye appeal. Deliciously flavored with the sauce or dip it houses, the bowl becomes an edible serving dish that is enjoyed right along with the meal.

Typically, holiday tables are filled with the same traditional favorites year after year because, after all, we love them! And because we are so used to preparing the usual standbys, we may neglect to add anything new. To help you think outside the box, this chapter offers a variety of great-tasting dishes to serve alongside (or perhaps instead of) those tried-and-true holiday regulars. Housing them in bread bowls further adds to their distinction. Ring in the New Year with Champagne Chicken a l'Orange—a good luck toast never tasted so good! Try the Sweet Potato Shepherd's Pie or Sir George's Royal Cranberry Sauce along with your Thanksgiving turkey. Grace your holiday table with Chef Salvatore John Campagna's Christmas Tenderloin—a flavorful mélange of juicy steak and assorted vegetables in a magnificent Cabernet sauce. The list goes on and on.

It is our prediction that the taste-tempting bread bowl dishes in this chapter will quickly join your list of traditional holiday favorites. Don't be surprised if you find yourself serving them all year long.

NEW YEAR'S CHAMPAGNE CHICKEN AL'ORANGE

Nothing shouts "Happy New Year" louder than a champagne toast. We put champagne to even better use as part of this delicious chicken entrée.

YIELD: 4 SERVINGS

3 boneless chicken breast halves

¼ teaspoon salt

¼ teaspoon black pepper

1½ cups cooked white rice

1- to 1¾-pound bread bowl

SAUCE

⅓ cup frozen orange juice concentrate

¼ cup champagne

2 tablespoons butter

½ teaspoon ground ginger

1. Preheat the oven to 375°F. Spray a medium-sized baking pan with nonstick cooking spray.

2. Combine the sauce ingredients in a small saucepan, and simmer over low heat. When well-blended and heated through, turn off the heat.

3. Sprinkle the chicken with salt and pepper, and place in the baking pan skin side up. Bake for 35 minutes, then cover with the sauce. Continue to bake another 20 minutes, or until the chicken is no longer pink inside when cut with a knife. Remove the chicken from the oven and cut into bite-sized pieces. Reduce the oven temperature to 350°F.

4. Spoon the rice in the bottom of the bread bowl. Top with the chicken and sauce.

5. Wrap the bowl with aluminum foil, leaving the top uncovered. Place the bowl on a baking sheet in the middle of the oven, and bake for 12 minutes or until heated through. Carefully remove the foil and continue to bake another 3 minutes. Serve hot.

SPICYLAMBEASTERBASKET

*A crisp sourdough bread bowl becomes a festive
Easter basket for this spicy lamb casserole that
is uniquely flavored with gingersnaps.*

YIELD: **4 SERVINGS**

1 ½ pounds ground lamb

¾ cup finely crushed
gingersnaps

1 ½ tablespoons soy sauce

1 teaspoon garlic powder

½ teaspoon curry powder

¼ teaspoon black pepper

1 ½ cups beef broth

¾ cup water

1 cup white rice

8-ounce can
stewed tomatoes

1- to 1¾-pound bread bowl

1. Combine the lamb, gingersnaps, soy sauce, garlic powder, curry powder, and pepper in a mixing bowl, then transfer to a medium skillet. Place over medium-low heat and brown until thoroughly cooked. Remove from the heat and set aside.

2. Preheat the oven to 350°F.

3. Bring the beef broth and water to boil in a medium saucepan. Stir in the rice, reduce the heat to low, and simmer covered for 15 minutes, or until the liquid is absorbed and the rice is tender.

4. Spoon the rice into the bread bowl, add the lamb, and top with tomatoes.

5. Wrap the bowl with aluminum foil, leaving the top uncovered. Place the bowl on a baking sheet in the middle of the oven, and bake for 12 minutes or until the filling is heated through. Carefully remove the foil and continue to bake another 3 minutes. Serve hot.

FOURTHOF**JULY**
CHILI**DOG**CASSEROLE

A juicy hot dog topped with meaty chili, sautéed onions, and melted cheese is one of life's guilty pleasures. Our Independence Day casserole is a tribute to this summertime favorite.

YIELD: 4 SERVINGS

6 all-beef hot dogs

I tablespoon butter

I small onion, cut into rings then halved

3 cups prepared chili con carne with beans

I ½ teaspoons prepared mustard

I teaspoon caraway seeds

¾ cup shredded Monterey pepperjack cheese, or plain Monterey Jack

I- to I ¾-pound bread bowl

1. Preheat the oven to 350°F.

2. Grill, broil, or boil the hot dogs according to package directions. Slice diagonally into bite-sized pieces, and set aside.

3. Melt the butter in a medium skillet over medium-low heat. Add the onion and sauté 10 minutes, or until brown and caramelized. Remove from the heat and set aside.

4. Spoon the chili con carne, hot dogs, mustard, and caraway seeds in the bread bowl, and mix gently.

5. Wrap the bowl with aluminum foil, leaving the top uncovered. Place the bowl on a baking sheet in the middle of the oven, and bake for 15 minutes. Sprinkle the onions and cheese on top, and bake another 10 minutes. Carefully remove the foil and continue to bake another 3 minutes. Serve hot.

TURKEY-CRANBERRY**POT**PIE

*Crisp sourdough bread replaces traditional piecrust in
this day-after-Thanksgiving salute to leftovers.*

YIELD: 4 SERVINGS

3 cups chicken broth

I carrot, diced

2 red potatoes,
cut into ½-inch cubes

2 stalks celery, diced

4 tablespoons (½ stick) butter

¼ cup diced onion

½ cup thinly sliced
mushrooms

½ teaspoon dried sage

½ teaspoon dried marjoram

Salt, to taste

Black pepper, to taste

3 tablespoons
all-purpose flour

3 tablespoons heavy cream

3 cups diced cooked turkey

¼ cup frozen peas, thawed

¼ cup whole berry
cranberry sauce

I- to I ¾-pound bread bowl

1. Preheat the oven to 350°F.

2. Simmer the broth in a medium saucepan over medium-low heat. Add the carrot, potatoes, and celery, and cook for 15 minutes, or until just tender. Reserving the broth, drain the vegetables and set aside.

3. In the same saucepan, melt the butter over medium-low heat. Add the onion, and sauté for 4 minutes, or until soft and translucent. Add the mushrooms, and cook another 2 minutes, then add the sage, marjoram, salt, and pepper.

4. Stirring constantly, add the flour to the saucepan, then slowly add the cream and reserved broth. Continue stirring until thickened. Add the cooked vegetables, turkey, peas, and cranberry sauce.

5. Spoon the mixture into the bread bowl. Wrap the bowl with aluminum foil, leaving the top uncovered. Place the bowl on a baking sheet in the middle of the oven, and bake for 12 minutes or until the filling is heated through. Carefully remove the foil and continue to bake another 3 minutes. Serve hot.

SWEET**POTATO**SHEPHERD'S**PIE**

Brown sugar sweet and cinnamony good,
mashed sweet potatoes crown this vegetable shepherd's pie
for a memorable Thanksgiving Day side dish.

YIELD: 6 SERVINGS

2 tablespoons olive oil

1 medium onion, chopped

1 tablespoon all-purpose flour

1 cup chicken broth

3 cups bite-sized mixed
vegetables: carrots, celery,
broccoli, cauliflower,
and thawed frozen peas

¼ teaspoon salt

¼ teaspoon black pepper

¼ teaspoon dried sage

¼ teaspoon dried marjoram

1- to 1¾-pound bread bowl

SWEET POTATO TOPPING

1 pound sweet potatoes,
peeled and cut into
large chunks

1 tablespoon butter

2 tablespoons brown sugar

¼ teaspoon ground nutmeg

¼ teaspoon ground
cinnamon

1. Boil the potatoes in a saucepan over medium heat for 20 minutes or until tender. Drain and transfer to a large bowl along with the butter, brown sugar, nutmeg, and cinnamon. Mash until smooth. Cover and set aside.

2. Preheat the oven to 350°F.

3. Heat the oil in a large deep skillet over medium heat. Add the onion and sauté for 4 minutes, or until soft and translucent. Stirring constantly, add the flour a little at a time to form a thick paste. Slowly add the broth, continuing to stir until thickened.

4. Add the mixed vegetables, salt, pepper, sage, and marjoram to the skillet, increase the heat, and bring to a boil. Reduce heat to low, simmer 8 minutes, then remove from the heat.

5. Spoon the vegetable mixture into the bread bowl and top with the sweet potatoes.

6. Wrap the bowl with aluminum foil, leaving the top uncovered. Place the bowl on a baking sheet in the middle of the oven, and bake for 12 minutes or until the filling is heated through. Carefully remove the foil and continue to bake another 3 minutes. Serve hot.

SIR**GEORGE'S**ROYAL **CRANBERRY**SAUCE

This luscious cranberry sauce, with its bits of orange, apple, and pineapple, is the one made famous by Sir George's Royal Buffet family restaurant, owned by Lisa's parents. They are asked to bring this sauce to every Thanksgiving dinner.

YIELD: 10 SERVINGS

2 packages (6-ounces each) raspberry gelatin

2 oranges, peeled and halved

2 teaspoons orange zest

2 apples, unpeeled, halved, and cored

1 ½ cups whole berry cranberry sauce

¾ cup crushed canned pineapple, drained

1- to 1 ¾-pound bread bowl

1. Prepare the gelatin according to package directions, but only until the gelatin is dissolved—do not add any additional water. Remove from the heat and set aside.

2. Place the oranges, zest, apples, and ½ cup of the cranberry sauce in a food processor, and pulse until chopped into pea-sized chunks. Transfer to a large bowl.

3. Add the pineapple, gelatin, and remaining cranberry sauce to the bowl. Gently mix the ingredients together, but do not over mix. Refrigerate until set.

4. Gently break up the gelled cranberry mixture with a spoon, transfer to the bread bowl, and serve.

CHEF**SALVATORE**JOHN
CAMPAGNA'SCHRISTMAS
TENDERLOIN

In addition to being a consulting chef for the San Francisco 49ers, Salvatore John Campagna, past president, Chef-of-the-Year, and medal winner of the Chefs Association of the Pacific Coast, is also the owner of Salvatore's restaurant in the San Francisco Bay area. He considers this dish one of his holiday favorites.

Yield: 4 servings

- I asparagus spear, no more than ½-inch in diameter
- I thin carrot, no more than ½-inch in diameter
- 2 large Swiss chard leaves, with white bottoms removed
- 2 long red bell pepper strips
- 4 cups beef broth
- 4 cups vegetable broth
- I small yellow onion, coarsely chopped
- I large carrot, coarsely chopped
- 2 stalks celery, coarsely chopped
- 24-ounce center-cut beef tenderloin roast, trimmed
- I tablespoon vegetable oil
- ½ cup Cabernet Sauvignon, or other dry red wine
- I tablespoon cornstarch
- 1- to 1¾-pound bread bowl

1. Blanch the asparagus, carrot, and Swiss chard leaves. When cool enough to handle, lay the chard leaves on top of each other, and place the asparagus, carrot, and bell pepper strips in a straight line along the center. Tightly wrap the vegetables in the leaves to form a cylinder. Cover tightly with plastic wrap, and freeze at least 4 hours.

2. Place the beef broth, vegetable broth, onion, carrot, and celery in a large stockpot over medium-low heat, and simmer for 2 hours.

3. Preheat the oven to 375°F.

4. With long sharp knife, make a deep ½-inch-wide slit in the center of each end of the roast. (The cuts from each end should meet in the middle of the roast.) Enlarge the slit with the handle of a wooden spoon. Remove the plastic wrap from the frozen Swiss chard "spear," then force the spear into the slit.

5. Heat the oil in a large ovenproof skillet over medium heat. Add the tenderloin, and brown on all sides. Remove the excess oil, and place the roast (still in the skillet) in the oven for 20 minutes, or until cooked to desired doneness. Remove the roast from the oven, transfer to a platter, and let sit at least 10 minutes. Reduce the oven temperature to 350°F.

6. Place the skillet over low heat, add half the wine, and stir to deglaze the pan. Add 4 cups of the simmering broth and cook 7 minutes, or until the liquid is reduced by a quarter.

7. Dissolve the cornstarch in the remaining wine, and add to the broth. Stir frequently until slightly thickened to form a sauce (Cabernet Jus Lie).

8. If necessary, trim the edges of the roast, so that it will easily fit in the bread bowl. Cut the roast into slices, but keep the slices together to maintain the "roast" shape. Transfer to the bread bowl. Add ¾ cup of the sauce, reserving the rest to serve at the table.

9. Wrap the bowl with aluminum foil, leaving the top uncovered. Place the bowl on a baking sheet in the middle of the oven, and bake for 5 minutes or until heated through. Carefully remove the foil and continue to bake another 3 minutes. Serve immediately.

HAM**AND**GREEN**BEAN**CASSEROLE

*Layers of tender sweet ham are nestled between
creamy mushroom-studded green beans and topped with
savory croutons in this favorite Christmas side dish.*

YIELD: 6 SERVINGS

10.75-ounce can cream
of mushroom soup

¾ cup milk

⅛ teaspoon black pepper

4 cups cooked green beans

3 cups bite-sized cubes
glazed ham

1- to 1¾-pound
bread bowl

CROUTONS

3 tablespoons unsalted
butter

1½ cups ½-inch bread
cubes from the
hollowed-out bowl

1½ teaspoons onion powder

1 teaspoon curry powder

1. Preheat the oven to 350°F. Coat a 1½-quart casserole dish with cooking spray, and set aside.

2. Combine the soup, milk, and pepper in a medium bowl, add the beans, and transfer to the casserole dish. Bake for 25 minutes, or until slightly bubbling.

3. While the beans bake, prepare the croutons. Heat the butter in a medium skillet over medium heat until it foams (do not burn). Add the bread cubes and toss to coat. Arrange the cubes on a baking sheet, and sprinkle with onion and curry powder. Place in the oven for 15 minutes, stirring the cubes a few times as they bake. Remove when they are brown on the outside, but soft on the inside.

4. Place half the ham on the bottom of the bread bowl, and top with half the green beans. Repeat the layers and top with croutons.

5. Wrap the bowl with aluminum foil, leaving the top uncovered. Place the bowl on a baking sheet in the middle of the oven, and bake for 12 minutes or until the filling is heated through. Carefully remove the foil and continue to bake another 3 minutes. Serve hot.

3.Appetizer
Delights

Spinach dip served in a sourdough bread bowl has become almost as American as apple pie. What Super Bowl party, potluck dinner, or buffet table is without it? Believe it or not, John was instrumental in its creation. In 1985, while working in sales for a major sourdough bread company, he became part of a team that created the now famous "spinach dip appetizer" as a winning supermarket promotion for that year's Super Bowl. The idea of carving out a sourdough round and filling it with a luscious dip scored an instant touchdown with the public.

Since then dips and spreads of all types have become popular fillings for millions of bread bowls, and in this chapter, we serve up some spectacular ones. There is our very own spinach dip made with juicy bits of portabella mushrooms and chopped pine nuts, a Warm Baja Shrimp Taco Dip that is enhanced with lime salsa, and a Caramelized Onion and Blue Cheese Dip for all of those onion lovers out there.

In addition to dips, we offer innovative recipes for appetizers that bask beautifully in bread bowls. There is the spicy Buffalo Wing Appetizer, Cocktail Weenie Bowl with a flavorful baked bean sauce, and a gingery Teriyaki Chicken Bowl complete with glazed chicken and rice. And from San Francisco's famous Farallon's restaurant, there's the delectable Crab Imperial Gratin. Outstanding!

Not only will you be amazed at the variety of appetizer-type foods you can put into bread bowls, you are bound to have lots of fun making and serving them to family and friends.

SPINACH**DIP**WITH**PORTABELLA** **MUSHROOMS**AND**PINE**NUTS

Sautéed portabella mushrooms and ground pine nuts lend a flavorful dimension to this spinach dip, which always gets rave reviews.

YIELD: 8 SERVINGS

2 tablespoons olive oil

1/4 cup chopped onions

2 cloves garlic, thinly sliced

3/4 cup minced portabella mushrooms

10-ounce package frozen chopped spinach, thawed and well drained

1/4 cup ground pine nuts

1 1/2 cups heavy cream

1/4 cup cream cheese, softened

1/4 teaspoon salt

1/4 teaspoon black pepper

1/4 cup freshly grated Parmesan cheese

Bread from the hollowed-out bowl for dipping

1- to 1 3/4-pound bread bowl

1. Heat the oil in a large skillet over medium heat.

2. Add the onions and garlic, reduce the heat to low, and sauté about 2 minutes, or until the onions are translucent. Add the mushrooms, spinach, and pine nuts, and continue to sauté an additional 2 minutes.

3. Add the cream, cream cheese, salt, and pepper to the skillet, and gently stir until the cream cheese is melted and the mixture is well blended.

4. Remove from the heat and stir in the Parmesan cheese.

5. Spoon the warm dip into the bread bowl. Serve with pieces of sourdough bread.

WARMBAJASHRIMP TACODIP

Vendors on the streets of Baja, Mexico, are known for their legendary seafood tacos, which inspired us to create this unique dip—a perfect complement to sourdough bread.

1. Heat the oil in a large skillet over medium heat.

2. Add the scallions and garlic, reduce the heat to low, and sauté for 1 minute. Add the shrimp and continue to sauté another minute.

3. Transfer the shrimp mixture to a large bowl. Add all of the remaining ingredients except the cabbage and bread, and mix gently until well blended. Fold in the cabbage.

4. Spoon the warm dip into the bread bowl. Serve with pieces of sourdough bread.

YIELD: 8 SERVINGS

2 tablespoons olive oil

1/4 cup chopped scallions

1 clove garlic, thinly sliced

12 ounces cooked shrimp, chopped

3/4 cup mayonnaise

3/4 cup sour cream

1/4 cup coarsely chopped cilantro, loosely packed

2 tablespoons finely chopped jalapeño or serrano pepper*

1 tablespoon lime juice

1/4 teaspoon salt

1/4 teaspoon white pepper

3/4 cup shredded fresh cabbage

Bread from the hollowed-out bowl for dipping

1- to 1 3/4-pound bread bowl

*When chopping the peppers, be sure to wear gloves, and be careful not to touch your eyes.

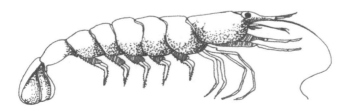

CARAMELIZED**ONION**AND **BLUE**CHEESE**DIP**

*Pungent blue cheese and sweet caramelized onions
add a flavorful spark to this positively addictive dip
that is baked right in the bowl.*

YIELD: 8 SERVINGS

I tablespoon butter

I medium onion, thinly cut
into rings and halved

I ½ cups crumbled
blue cheese

I cup cream cheese,
softened

½ cup sour cream

I teaspoon black pepper

Bread from the hollowed-out
bowl for dipping

I- to I ¾-pound bread bowl

1. Preheat the oven to 350°F.

2. Melt the butter in a medium-sized skillet over medium-low heat. Add the onion and sauté about 10 minutes, or until brown and caramelized. Remove from the heat and set aside.

3. Place the blue cheese, cream cheese, sour cream, and pepper in a food processor, and pulse until blended. Transfer to a medium bowl, add the onions, and stir until well combined.

4. Spoon the mixture into the bread bowl. Wrap the bowl with aluminum foil, leaving the top uncovered. Place the bowl on a baking sheet in the middle of the oven, and bake about 7 minutes or until the dip is heated through. Carefully remove the foil and continue to bake another 3 minutes.

5. Serve with pieces of sourdough bread.

THREE-**CHEESE**BALL **IN**A**BOWL**

Most cheese balls are made of one kind of cheese and rolled in chopped nuts (ho hum). In this unique bread bowl appetizer, thick layers of a Cheddar cheese, ricotta, and cream cheese blend are blanketed between crunchy tiers of walnuts, pecans, and hazelnuts.

1. In a large bowl, combine the Cheddar, cream cheese, ricotta, and sugar until well blended. Cover and refrigerate for 1 hour.

2. Combine the pecans, walnuts, and hazelnuts in a small bowl and set aside.

3. Spread ¼ cup of the cheese mixture on the bottom of the bread bowl. Sprinkle ⅓ of the nut mixture on top. Next, add a layer of the cheese mixture, using half of the remaining cheese, and top with half of the remaining nuts. Repeat layers with the rest of the cheese and nuts.

4. Serve with toasted sourdough bread.

YIELD: 8 SERVINGS

16 ounces sharp Cheddar cheese spread

8-ounce package cream cheese, softened

½ cup ricotta cheese

1 teaspoon sugar

½ cup chopped pecans

½ cup chopped walnuts

½ cup chopped hazelnuts

Bread from the hollowed-out bowl, cut into 2-inch squares and toasted

1- to 1¾-pound bread bowl

COCKTAIL WEENIE BOWL

*Old-fashioned appetizer-style cocktail weenies shivering
on toothpicks pale in comparison to those swimming in
this hot and bubbly bowl of special sauce and beans.*

YIELD: 8 SERVINGS

2 packages (16-ounces each)
all-beef hot dogs

8-ounce can tomato sauce

¾ cup water

1.5-ounce package
spaghetti sauce mix

2 tablespoons vegetable oil

2 tablespoons instant coffee

¼ teaspoon cayenne pepper

½ cup baked beans

1 ½ teaspoons honey

Bread from the hollowed-out
bowl, cut into chunks

1- to 1 ¾-pound bread bowl

1. Grill, broil, or boil the hot dogs according to package directions. Slice diagonally into bite-sized pieces and set aside.

2. In a large saucepan, combine the tomato sauce, water, spaghetti sauce mix, vegetable oil, coffee, and cayenne pepper. Simmer over low heat for 5 minutes.

3. Add the hot dogs, baked beans, and honey. Increase the heat to medium-low and simmer about 5 minutes, or until slightly bubbling and heated through.

4. Pour the mixture into the bread bowl. Spoon portions onto individual plates and eat with forks. Serve with chunks of sourdough bread.

BUFFALOWINGAPPETIZER

This dish is a tribute to Buffalo, New York, where spicy Buffalo chicken wings originated. The sauce, which includes crunchy celery and a swirl of blue cheese dressing, is the perfect complement to its sourdough bread container.

YIELD: 8 SERVINGS

2 pounds chicken wings

3 cups vegetable oil
for deep-frying

$1/4$ cup butter

4 tablespoons Tabasco sauce

$1/4$ cup blue cheese dressing

$3/4$ cup chopped celery

Bread from the hollowed-out
bowl, cut into chunks

Additional squares of
sourdough bread

1-pound to 1$3/4$-pound
bread bowl

1. Wash the chicken wings and pat dry with paper towels. Separate them at the joints, discard the small tips, and set aside.

2. Heat the oil in a large saucepan over medium-high heat. Carefully fry the wings about 10 minutes or until crisp. Remove with a slotted spoon and drain on paper towels. Once cool, remove the meat from the bones, leaving the skin intact. Discard the bones.

3. Melt the butter in a large saucepan over medium heat, and stir in the Tabasco sauce. Reduce the heat to low, add the chicken, and toss to coat. Add the blue cheese dressing, celery, and chunks of sourdough. Mix together gently.

4. Spoon the warm mixture into the bread bowl. Serve over squares of sourdough bread on individual plates.

CHICKEN
PARMIGIANA**HERO**

This appetizing version of the classic Italian sandwich is guaranteed to draw rave reviews. Its tantalizing aroma will transform your kitchen into an Italian trattoria.

YIELD: **8** SERVINGS

SAUCE

2 pints red grape tomatoes*

¾ cup water

2 tablespoons dried oregano

I teaspoon dried minced onion, or ½ teaspoon onion powder

½ teaspoon salt

½ teaspoon black pepper

¼ teaspoon garlic powder

4 tablespoons sour cream

---

*You can also use 4 large plum tomatoes, diced and sprinkled with 1 ¼ teaspoons sugar or granulated fructose.

1. Place all of the sauce ingredients, except the sour cream, in a blender or food processor, and blend to a slightly chunky consistency. Pour into a medium microwave-safe container and set aside in the refrigerator.

2. Preheat the oven to 350°F.

3. Place all of the chicken ingredients in a large bowl and stir until well blended

4. Spray a large nonstick skillet with cooking spray, add the olive oil, and heat over medium heat. Add the chicken mixture and cook, stirring often, for 8 to 10 minutes, or until the meat is crumbly and cooked through. Remove from the heat and set aside.

5. Remove the sauce from the refrigerator, add the sour cream, and stir gently. Heat in the microwave oven for 3½ minutes on high power. Remove and stir carefully.

6. Transfer the chicken mixture to the bread bowl. Add the sauce, and top with the mozzarella and Parmesan. Place the bowl on a baking sheet in the center of the oven and heat for 2 minutes, or until the cheeses are melting and bubbly.

7. Spoon portions onto individual plates and eat with forks. Serve with pieces of sourdough bread.

CHICKEN MIXTURE

1 pound ground chicken

1 tablespoon dried minced onion, or 1 ½ teaspoons onion powder

1 tablespoon dried oregano

1 teaspoon fennel seed

½ teaspoon allspice

½ teaspoon salt

½ teaspoon black pepper

¼ teaspoon garlic powder

ADDITIONAL INGREDIENTS

1 tablespoon olive oil

¾ cup shredded mozzarella cheese

¼ cup shredded Parmesan cheese

Bread from the hollowed-out bowl, cut into chunks

1- to 1¾-pound bread bowl

YIAYIA'SMEATBALLBOWL

*John's mother Emily ("Yia Yia" to her grandkids) is a
longtime professional cook whose Greek heritage has greatly
influenced her cooking. It was only a matter of time before
her mouth-watering meatballs and sauce found
their way into a sourdough bread bowl.*

YIELD: **8 SERVINGS**

MEATBALLS

1 pound ground chuck

1 medium yellow onion,
minced

1 egg

³/₄ cup breadcrumbs*

¹/₃ cup ketchup

1 teaspoon cumin

Dash cinnamon

Salt, to taste

White pepper, to taste

---

*To make breadcrumbs from the
hollowed-out bowl, see page 13.

1. Preheat the oven to 350°F. Lightly oil a baking sheet and set
aside.

2. To make the meatballs, place the ground chuck, onion, egg,
breadcrumbs, ketchup, cumin, cinnamon, salt, and pepper
in a mixing bowl and mix until smooth and well-blended.
Form the mixture into meatballs the size of ping-pong balls,
and arrange on the baking sheet.

3. Bake the meatballs for 10 minutes. Turn them over, and continue to bake an additional 10 minutes, or until they are
cooked through completely. Transfer to paper towels to
drain.

4. While the meatballs bake, prepare the sauce. Place the olive
oil in a large saucepan over medium-low heat. Add the garlic and sauté about 1 minute or until it browns. Remove the
garlic with a slotted spoon and discard.

5. Add the purée, water, vinegar, sugar, oregano, and bay leaves to the saucepan. Simmer for 25 minutes while stirring occasionally. Remove and discard the bay leaves. Carefully add the cooled meatballs to the sauce and continue to simmer another 10 minutes.

6. Transfer the warm meatballs and sauce to the bread bowl, and sprinkle with Parmesan cheese. Spoon portions onto individual plates and eat with forks. Serve with pieces of sourdough bread.

SAUCE

3 tablespoons olive oil

2 cloves garlic, minced

1 ½ cups tomato purée

1 cup water

¼ cup cider vinegar or red wine vinegar

¼ cup sugar

1 tablespoon oregano

2 bay leaves

ADDITIONAL INGREDIENTS

2 tablespoons freshly grated Parmesan cheese

Bread from the hollowed-out bowl, cut into chunks

1- to 1¾-pound bread bowl

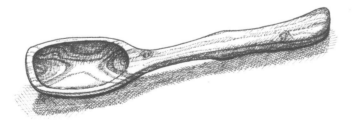

FARALLON'SCRAB IMPERIALGRATIN

This popular dish is served at San Francisco's highly acclaimed Farallon restaurant, which is known for its innovative seafood recipes. Executive chef and co-owner, Mark Franz, serves this deviled crab casserole in ramekins, which patrons enjoy with sourdough bread. We use a bread bowl to house his famous masterpiece—a perfect match!

YIELD: 8 SERVINGS

3 medium red potatoes, peeled and diced

8 ounces fresh lump crabmeat (preferably Dungeness)

1 ½ tablespoons unsalted butter

½ cup fresh or frozen corn kernels

½ cup crème fraiche

1 tablespoon lemon zest

1 teaspoon chopped fresh tarragon

½ to 1 teaspoon white truffle oil or olive oil

Salt (preferably kosher), to taste

Black pepper, to taste

4 sprigs tarragon or thyme for garnish

Bread from the hollowed-out bowl, cut into chunks

1-pound to 1¾-pound bread bowl

1. In a small saucepan, cook the potatoes in salted boiling water about 5 minutes, or until barely tender. Drain and set aside.

2. Place the crabmeat in a medium bowl and set aside.

3. In a small skillet, melt the butter over low heat. Add the corn and cook about 3 minutes, or until soft. Transfer the corn to the bowl with the crabmeat. Add the potatoes, crème fraiche, lemon zest, tarragon, oil, salt, and pepper. Stir the ingredients until thoroughly combined. Set aside.

4. Preheat the oven to 400°F.

5. To prepare the breadcrumb topping, melt the butter in a small skillet over medium heat. Add the breadcrumbs and thyme, and cook, stirring often, for 2 to 3 minutes, or until the crumbs are golden brown. Season with salt and pepper, and set aside.

6. Spoon the crab mixture into the bread bowl, top with an even layer of breadcrumbs, and drizzle with a little oil. Wrap the bowl with aluminum foil, leaving the top uncovered. Place the bowl on a baking sheet in the middle of the oven, and bake for 7 minutes or until heated through. Remove the foil and continue to bake another 3 minutes.

7. Before serving, garnish with tarragon. Spoon portions onto individual plates and eat with forks. Serve with pieces of sourdough bread.

BREADCRUMB TOPPING

1 tablespoon unsalted butter

$\frac{1}{2}$ cup breadcrumbs*

$\frac{1}{2}$ teaspoon chopped fresh thyme, or $\frac{1}{4}$ teaspoon dried

Salt (preferably kosher), to taste

Black pepper, to taste

White truffle oil or extra-virgin olive oil for drizzling

---

*To make breadcrumbs from the hollowed-out bowl, see page 13.

TERIYAKICHICKEN**BOWL**

A sprinkling of ginger gives this bowl of teriyaki-glazed chicken and steamed rice added zest. In addition to making a great appetizer, this dish can serve as a light lunch or dinner.

YIELD: 8 SERVINGS

1 cup soy sauce

1 ¼ cups sugar

3 cloves garlic, minced

2-inch piece fresh ginger,
peeled and sliced,
or 1 teaspoon ground

1 tablespoon dry sherry

1 ½ teaspoons vegetable oil

3 cooked skinless
chicken breasts, cut into
1-x-2-inch slices

2 cups cooked white rice

Bread from the hollowed-out
bowl, cut into chunks

1- to 1¾-pound bread bowl

1. In a medium saucepan, combine the soy sauce and sugar. Place over low heat and gently stir about 1 minute or until the sugar dissolves.

2. Add the garlic, ginger, sherry, and oil. Simmer for 20 minutes, stirring occasionally. With a slotted spoon, carefully remove and discard the garlic and ginger.

3. Add the chicken and rice to the pan, and mix together gently. Continue to simmer for 10 minutes.

4. Transfer the mixture to the bread bowl. To serve, spoon portions onto individual plates and eat with forks. Enjoy with pieces of sourdough bread.

4.Let's**Have** Brunch**!**

Sleeping in late on your day off is one of life's simple pleasures. Enjoying a leisurely brunch with family and friends is another. Often served buffet-style, brunch can include a selection of basic food choices, elaborate gourmet dishes, or a delectable combination of both. One thing is certain, whether simple or gourmet, a brunch-style dish served in an edible bread bowl makes a wonderful presentation, and its "one-dish" appeal adds to the communal feeling of the gathering.

If the bread-bowl brunch concept is new to you, we welcome you into the fold with some of our all-time favorite recipes. Eggs, whether scrambled, poached, or served up as fluffy omelets, are staple offerings at this special meal. Our egg-inspired contributions include Bread-Bowl Quiche Lorraine, Mexican-style Juevos Rancheros, and a BLT Omelet that is layered into the bread bowl, then cut into wedges and served. Chef Bren Boyd also offers his San Francisco-Style Eggs Sardou—a New Orleans classic with a decidedly West Coast twist.

In addition to egg dishes, you'll find other terrific brunch recipes. There are savory creations like Brunch-Style Chili, and lighter fare such as the Strawberry-Blintz Casserole. For those who like nut breads and coffeecake, the Banana-Yogurt Bread Bowl is an excellent choice as is the Peaches 'n' Cream Coffeecake Crumble. Mmmmmmm.

Brunch is a time for relaxing and enjoying the company of others—for savoring good food amid fun and fellowship! Choosing from among these recipes will help you create the perfect menu for your event.

BLT BREAD BOWL OMELET

Honey-glazed Canadian bacon, mixed salad greens,
and sun-dried tomatoes are nestled between omelet layers
in a crunchy bread bowl for a special brunch offering.

YIELD: 4 SERVINGS

12 ounces Canadian bacon, cut
into bite-sized cubes

2 tablespoons honey

2 teaspoons chopped
fresh rosemary

6 eggs, beaten

4 cups mixed salad greens

1 cup sun-dried tomatoes,
drained and chopped

1 cup halved black olives

Chopped rosemary for garnish

1- to 1¾-pound bread bowl

1. Preheat the oven to 350°F. Lightly coat a medium skillet with nonstick cooking spray, and place over medium-low heat. Add the Canadian bacon, honey, and rosemary, and cook about 2 minutes. Transfer to a dish and set aside.

2. Clean the skillet, coat with more cooking spray, and place over medium heat. When the skillet is hot, add half the eggs. Cook about 2 minutes, or until the bottom of the eggs are set. Carefully flip the omelet over and continue to cook until another 2 minutes, or until completely cooked. Transfer the omelet to a platter, and prepare a second omelet with the remaining eggs.

3. Place one omelet on the bottom of the bread bowl. Top with half the salad greens, Canadian bacon, tomatoes, and olives. Add the second omelet and top with the remaining greens, bacon, tomatoes, and olives.

4. Wrap the bowl with aluminum foil, leaving the top uncovered. Place the bowl on a baking sheet in the middle of the oven, and bake for 12 minutes or until the filling is heated through. Carefully remove the foil and continue to bake another 3 minutes.

5. Garnish with rosemary, cut into wedges, and serve.

JUEVOS**RANCHEROS**

*Although traditionally wrapped in a warm tortilla,
this spicy Mexican egg-and-bean dish works just as well
(if not better) when housed in a sourdough bread bowl,
which deliciously absorbs the flavorful sauce.*

1. Preheat the oven to 350°F.

2. To prepare the vegetable-bean mixture, heat the olive oil in a large skillet over medium heat. Add the onion, garlic, red and green bell peppers, cumin, chile powder, and oregano, and cook about 5 minutes, or until the onion and peppers are soft.

3. Add the tomatoes, beans, chorizo, salt, and pepper to the skillet. Simmer for 15 minutes, or until most of the liquid has evaporated.

4. Crack the eggs into the simmering vegetable mixture, leaving room between them. Cover and cook about 5 minutes, or until the eggs are cooked through. Sprinkle with cheese, reduce the heat to low, and heat about 1 minute or until the cheese begins to melt.

5. While the eggs are cooking, heat the bread bowl in the oven for 3 minutes.

6. Scoop the hot juevos rancheros into the bread bowl along with any liquid. Serve immediately with salsa and cilantro sour cream on the side.

YIELD: 4 SERVINGS

6 eggs

$1/2$ cup shredded
Monterey Jack cheese

1- to $1\,3/4$-pound bread bowl

VEGETABLE-BEAN MIXTURE

1 tablespoon olive oil

1 small onion, chopped

2 cloves garlic, minced

$1/2$ cup finely chopped
red bell pepper

$1/2$ cup finely chopped
green bell pepper

$1/2$ teaspoon ground cumin

$1/2$ teaspoon chile powder

$1/2$ teaspoon oregano

1 cup chopped fresh tomatoes

1 cup cooked black beans

$1/2$ cup diced chorizo sausage

1 teaspoon salt

$1/4$ teaspoon black pepper

ACCOMPANIMENTS

1 cup salsa

$3/4$ cup sour cream mixed with
1 tablespoon dried cilantro

BREAD**BOWL** **QUICHE**LORRAINE

Rustic sourdough bread deliciously rivals the French pastry crust traditionally used for this classic quiche.

8 ounces Canadian bacon, cut into bite-sized cubes

4 eggs

2 cups heavy cream

½ teaspoon salt

¼ teaspoon black pepper

¼ teaspoon ground nutmeg

½ cup shredded Swiss cheese

½ cup chopped onion

1- to 1¾-pound bread bowl

1. Preheat the oven to 400°F.

2. Place the Canadian bacon in a medium skillet over medium heat, and cook about 2 minutes, or until slightly browned. Remove from the heat and set aside.

3. In a medium bowl, beat together the eggs, cream, salt, pepper, and nutmeg.

4. Sprinkle the bacon, cheese, and onion over the bottom of the bread bowl. Top with the egg mixture.

5. Wrap the bowl with aluminum foil, leaving the top uncovered. Place the bowl on a baking sheet in the middle of the oven, and bake for 30 minutes or until a knife inserted into the middle of the egg comes out clean. Carefully remove the foil and continue to bake another 3 minutes.

6. Cut the bread bowl into wedges and serve.

BRUNCH-STYLE**CHILI**

*This traditional chili becomes "brunch worthy" with the added
flavors from breakfast sausage and maple syrup.*

1. Preheat the oven broiler.

2. Brown the ground beef and sausage in a large pot over medium heat until no pink remains. Remove the fat. Add enough water to cover the meat, and bring to a boil.

3. Add the tomatoes, celery, onion, garlic, jalapeño and chipotle peppers, maple syrup, and chile powder to the pot. Reduce the heat to low. Stirring occasionally, simmer over low heat about 15 minutes, adding water as necessary to maintain a stew-like consistency.

4. Increase the heat, bring the ingredients to a boil, and add the beans. Continue to simmer another 20 minutes.

5. Spoon the chili into the bread bowl and serve.

YIELD: 6 SERVINGS

12 ounces ground beef

12 ounces ground breakfast sausage

5 large fresh tomatoes, chopped

2 stalks celery, chopped

1 medium yellow onion, chopped

2 cloves garlic, minced

4 jalapeño peppers, seeded and finely chopped*

2 chipotle peppers, finely chopped

2 tablespoons pure maple syrup

1 teaspoon chile powder

1 1/2 cups canned red kidney beans

1- to 1 3/4-pound bread bowl

*When preparing the peppers, be sure to wear gloves, and be careful not to touch your eyes.

STRAWBERRY
BLINTZ**CASSEROLE**

*This easy-to-prepare casserole is a brunch-table favorite—
we call it a shortcut to paradise.*

YIELD: 4 SERVINGS

12 frozen cheese blintzes

6 eggs, beaten

½ cup orange juice

2 tablespoons sugar

1 teaspoon vanilla

2 cups sour cream

2 cups strawberry preserves

1- to 1¾-pound bread bowl

1. Preheat the oven to 350°F.

2. Arrange the blintzes in a well-oiled casserole dish or baking pan. Set aside.

3. Combine the eggs, orange juice, sugar, vanilla, and 1 cup of the sour cream. Evenly pour over the blintzes.

4. Bake the casserole for 1 hour, or until the top is brown and the egg mixture is thoroughly cooked. Remove from the oven and set aside.

5. Place the bread bowl in the oven and warm for 3 minutes. Remove and generously spread most of the preserves on the inside of the bowl, reserving the rest to serve with the blintzes.

6. Using a spatula, cut the casserole into large squares and place in the bread bowl. Serve with the remaining sour cream and strawberry preserves on the side.

BANANA-YOGURT
BREAD**BOWL**

*A luscious addition to any brunch table, this creamy
yogurt blend is topped with marinated bananas,
crunchy walnuts, and flavorful granola.*

1. Preheat the oven to 350°F.

2. Combine the apple juice and orange juice in a small baking
pan, and set aside. Slice the bananas in half lengthwise, and
then crosswise. Lay them in the apple-orange juice mixture,
and let marinate for 10 minutes. Turn over and marinate
another 10 minutes.

3. Place the brown sugar, butter, and half the cinnamon in a
medium skillet over low heat. Stir gently but constantly
until the sugar dissolves. Add the bananas and continue to
cook for 3 minutes, or until the bananas begin to soften and
brown. Add about ¼ cup of the fruit-juice marinade, and
continue to cook until the mixture is hot.

4. Place the bread bowl in the oven and warm for 3 minutes.

5. Combine the yogurt, nutmeg, allspice, cloves, and remaining cinnamon in a medium bowl, then spoon into the bread
bowl. Top with granola, walnuts, hot bananas, and 2 tablespoons of the reserved marinade before serving.

YIELD: 6 SERVINGS

½ cup apple juice

¼ cup orange juice

4 bananas

¾ cup brown sugar

¼ cup butter

1 teaspoon ground
cinnamon

2 cups vanilla yogurt

1 teaspoon ground
nutmeg

½ teaspoon ground
allspice

½ teaspoon ground
cloves

1 cup granola

¼ cup walnut pieces

1- to 1¾-pound bread bowl

CHEFBRENBOYD'S SANFRANCISCO-STYLE EGGSSARDOU

The owner of San Francisco's Caylen's Catering and chef of the city's Irish Cultural Center, Bren Boyd grew up in Louisiana. He gives his Eggs Sardou—a dish straight out of New Orleans— a San Francisco flair by replacing the usual ham with crabmeat.

YIELD: **4** SERVINGS

4 eggs

2 tablespoons butter

1 teaspoon chopped shallots

1 teaspoon chopped garlic

1/2 cup chopped cooked artichoke hearts

1 pound coarsely chopped spinach

Salt, to taste

Black pepper, to taste

Dash nutmeg

1/2 cup heavy cream

3/4 cup flaked crabmeat (preferably Dungeness)

1- to 1 3/4-pound bread bowl

1. To poach the eggs, bring a quart of water to boil in a large saucepan over high heat. Reduce the heat to low, then carefully crack the eggs into the water without breaking the yolks. Simmer gently (do not boil) about 5 minutes, or until the egg whites are opaque. Using a slotted spoon, transfer the cooked eggs to a warm plate, cover, and set aside.

2. While the eggs are cooking, melt the butter in a large skillet over medium-low heat. Add the shallots, garlic, and artichoke hearts, and sauté about 3 minutes, or until the shallots are soft and light brown. Add the spinach, salt, pepper, and nutmeg, continuing to sauté for 3 minutes, or until the spinach is wilted. Stirring occasionally, add the cream and continue to cook about 3 minutes, or until the liquid has thickened.

3. While the spinach mixture cooks, prepare the Hollandaise sauce. Combine the egg yolks, lemon juice, water, salt, pepper, and Tabasco sauce in the top half of a double boiler set over low heat. Whisk constantly until thick steam rises from the mixture, and the mixture begins to thicken. Slowly add the butter while stirring constantly.

4. Place the spinach mixture in the bottom of the bread bowl. Add the poached eggs, sprinkle with crabmeat, and top with the Hollandaise sauce. Serve hot.

HOLLANDAISE SAUCE

4 egg yolks

2 tablespoons fresh lemon juice

1 teaspoon water

Pinch salt

Pinch black pepper

Dash Tabasco sauce

2 sticks butter (8 ounces), melted

PEACHES'N'CREAM COFFEECAKECRUMBLE

For this easy-to-prepare brunch favorite, peaches, cream, and peach-flavored yogurt are nestled into a bread bowl lined with bite-sized morsels of coffee cake.

1. Gently combine the peaches, cream, and cinnamon in a medium bowl and set aside.

2. Press the coffeecake onto the bottom and sides of the bread bowl, then add the yogurt. Top with the peaches-and-cream mixture, gently stir, and serve.

YIELD: 6 SERVINGS

2 cups sliced fresh or canned peaches

1/2 cup heavy cream

1/2 teaspoon ground cinnamon

1 1/2 cups crumbled coffeecake with crumb topping

1 1/2 cups peach yogurt

1- to 1 3/4-pound bread bowl

HIT-THE-TRAIL-MIXPARFAIT

*Layers of honey-sweetened cottage cheese and crunchy
trail mix make up this memorable brunch parfait.*

YIELD: 6 SERVINGS

¼ cup honey

2 cups cottage cheese

1 teaspoon ground cinnamon

1 teaspoon ground allspice

2 cups trail mix

1- to 1¾-pound bread bowl

1. Heat the honey in a small pan over low heat about 1 minute.

2. Combine the cottage cheese, cinnamon, allspice, and warm honey in a bowl.

3. Spread half the cottage cheese mixture in the bread bowl, and top with half the trail mix. Repeat the layers, and serve.

CREAMYDATE-NUTSPREAD

*This scrumptious spread is a tribute to one of our all-time
favorite treats—cream cheese on date-nut bread.*

YIELD: 8 SERVINGS

3 packages (8-ounces each) cream cheese, softened

¼ cup brown sugar

1½ teaspoons cinnamon

1½ cups chopped dates

1½ cups chopped walnuts

Bread from hollowed-out bowl for spreading

1- to 1¾-pound bread bowl

1. In a medium bowl, combine the cream cheese, brown sugar, and cinnamon. Fold in the dates and walnuts.

2. Spoon the mixture into the bread bowl. Serve with pieces of bread.

5.The**Salad**Bowl

When it comes to sourdough bread bowl fillings, soups are the obvious stars with clam chowder leading the pack. Salads, on the other hand, have been firmly planted on the opposite end of the spectrum—pretty much overlooked, at least until now.

Think about it. What could be a better accompaniment for a fresh salad than a crust of hearty sourdough bread? Not much, unless, of course, the bread is actually part of the salad. Realizing that the inner walls of a bread bowl are able to absorb salad dressings just as deliciously as they soak up soups, John began to experiment. And it didn't take long for him to come up with an obvious winner—a magnificent creation of mixed baby greens, sliced pears, crumbled Roquefort, and candied walnuts christened with a blackberry balsamic vinaigrette (see page 52). After that, the salad ideas began to flow.

In this chapter, you'll find some of our favorite bread bowl salads for your eating pleasure—a diverse parade of outstanding recipes. If you're in the mood for cold seafood, the Crab Louis Salad, complete with a traditional spicy dressing will fill the bill. For a refreshing yet satisfying salad sensation, be sure to try the Mandarin Orange Chicken Salad, Indian Cucumber Raita, or Strawberry Fields Salad. And when it's a warm salad you're craving, the Sizzling Beef Fajita Salad served over a bed of warm spinach, or the Warm Cioppino Salad, inspired by Scoma's restaurant on Fisherman's Wharf, is sure to please.

Once you've made a few bread bowl salads, you'll be hooked. You'll also wonder how you ever set a table without them.

JOHN'S MIXED GREEN
MASTERPIECE

*A potpourri of mixed field greens and slices of sweet pear
form the base of this blue-ribbon salad, while crumbled
Roquefort cheese and candied walnuts offer added interest.
Although John uses aged blackberry balsamic vinegar for
the dressing, feel free to use your own favorite variety.*

YIELD: 4 SERVINGS

5 cups mixed salad greens,
such as arugula, frisee, red leaf,
romaine, red oak, and
butter lettuce

I Bosc pear, cored and
thinly sliced

1/2 cup crumbled
Roquefort cheese

1/2 cup candied walnuts
(see page 53)

I- to 1 3/4-pound bread bowl

DRESSING

2/3 cup extra-virgin olive oil

1/3 cup blackberry balsamic
vinegar, or other flavor

1/8 teaspoon salt

1/8 teaspoon black pepper

1. In a small bowl, lightly whisk together the dressing ingredients and set aside.

2. In a large bowl, add the greens, pear slices, cheese, and walnuts, and toss gently. Drizzle with one-third of the dressing, and toss again.

3. Transfer the salad to the bread bowl, and serve with the remaining dressing on the side.

Making Candied Nuts

*Candied nuts—walnuts, pecans, and cashews in particular—add welcomed flavor
and crunch to many types of salad. Adding to their appeal is that they require
only a few basic ingredients and are simple to prepare.*

1 cup granulated sugar

$1/2$ cup water

2 cups shelled nuts

Salt (optional)

1. Preheat the oven to 350°F. Lightly oil a baking sheet (or line with parchment paper) and set aside.

2. Combine the sugar and water in a small pan over medium-low heat. Cook the mixture while stirring for 10 minutes. Add the nuts, and continue to stir until the mixture begins to thicken and turn opaque.

3. Immediately spoon the sugar-coated nuts onto the cookie sheet. Using a fork, separate them into an even layer. Sprinkle lightly with salt, if using.

4. Bake for 10 minutes, then turn the nuts with a nonstick spatula. Cook another 10 minutes, or until the sugar has melted and the nuts are coated with brown sugary "syrup." Remove immediately and let cool. Store in an airtight container.

CRABLOUIS**SALAD**

Not many seafood dishes scream "San Francisco" louder than creamy Crab Louis. Traditionally tossed with a spicy dressing and served on a bed of lettuce, it's the perfect bread bowl filling.

YIELD: **4 SERVINGS**

1 ¼ pounds chilled crabmeat, separated into bite-sized pieces

½ head crisp iceberg lettuce, torn into bite-sized pieces

2 teaspoons chopped chives

1- to 1 ¾-pound bread bowl

DRESSING

½ cup mayonnaise

¼ cup chili sauce

1 tablespoon minced parsley

1 teaspoon vinegar

⅛ teaspoon horseradish

⅛ teaspoon Worcestershire sauce

1. In a small bowl, whisk together the dressing ingredients. Cover and refrigerate until chilled.

2. Spread 3 tablespoons of the chilled dressing on the inside of the bread bowl.

3. Place the crabmeat and lettuce in a large bowl, add the remaining dressing, and toss well.

4. Transfer the salad to the bread bowl, sprinkle with chives, and serve.

CALIFORNIA MANDARIN ORANGE CHICKEN SALAD

*Crystallized ginger adds a refreshing zing to
the fruity blend of mandarin oranges and
cranberries in this chilled chicken salad.*

YIELD: 4 SERVINGS

½ cup mayonnaise

1 ½ tablespoons honey

1 ½ teaspoons
crystallized ginger

3 cups diced cooked
chicken breasts

1 cup mandarin orange slices

¼ cup whole berry
cranberry sauce

¼ cup diced scallions

½ cups crisp chow mein
noodles

1- to 1 ¾-pound bread bowl

1. In a medium bowl, combine the mayonnaise, honey, and ginger. Add the chicken, oranges, cranberry sauce, and scallions, and stir until evenly coated. Cover and chill.

2. Spoon half the salad into the bread bowl, and top with half the chow mein noodles. Repeat the layers. Serve.

INDIAN**CUCUMBER**RAITA

Raita, or yogurt-based salad, is a staple of the Indian cuisine,
specifically created to tame the heat of the country's characteristic
spicy foods. Although Indian bread called naan usually
accompanies this salad, sourdough bread offers
the same delicious results.

YIELD: 6 SERVINGS

3 cups plain yogurt

3 cucumbers, seeded, finely
chopped, and squeezed dry

1/4 jalapeño pepper, seeded
and thinly sliced*

2 1/2 tablespoons chopped
fresh mint

1 1/4 teaspoon ground cumin

1 teaspoon salt

1/2 teaspoon ground coriander

1- to 1 3/4-pound bread bowl

---

*When preparing the pepper, be
sure to wear gloves, and be careful
not to touch your eyes.

1. Place all of the ingredients in a medium bowl and mix together gently. Transfer to an airtight container and refrigerate at least 4 hours or overnight.

2. Transfer the chilled raita to the bread bowl and serve.

STRAWBERRY FIELDS SALAD

Did you ever have strawberry jam on sourdough toast?
It's truly outstanding. The following salad is
refreshingly reminiscent of this toast treat.

YIELD: 4 SERVINGS

1. In a small bowl, lightly whisk together the French dressing, cayenne pepper, and black pepper. Set aside.

2. In a large bowl, add the strawberries, trail mix, lettuce, and 3 tablespoons of the dressing mixture. Toss gently.

3. Transfer the salad to the bread bowl, and serve with the remaining dressing on the side.

I cup French dressing

⅛ teaspoon cayenne pepper

⅛ teaspoon black pepper

1 ½ pints fresh strawberries, sliced

1 ½ cups trail mix with nuts and dried bananas

1 ½ cups romaine lettuce, torn into bite-sized pieces

1- to 1 ¾-pound bread bowl

ANTIPASTOBREADBOWL

¹⁄₄ head iceberg lettuce, torn into bite-sized pieces

4 ounces Italian salami, thickly sliced then cut into strips

4 ounces mortadella (Italian-style bologna), thickly sliced then cut into strips

4 ounces prosciutto, very thinly sliced, rolled up, and halved

4 ounces pepperoni, cut into thin circles

4 ounces mozzarella cheese, cut into bite-sized cubes

4 ounces provolone cheese, cut into bite-sized cubes

¹⁄₄ cup marinated artichoke hearts

¹⁄₄ cup pitted black olives

¹⁄₄ cup pimento-stuffed green olives

I cup Italian salad dressing

2 tablespoons freshly grated Parmesan cheese

I- to I ³⁄₄-pound bread bowl

Once you've enjoyed a delectable antipasto in a sourdough bread bowl, you'll never serve one on a plain old serving platter again.

1. Place the lettuce, salami, mortadella, prosciutto, pepperoni, mozzarella, provolone, artichoke hearts, and olives in a large bowl. Top with 5 tablespoons of dressing, and toss gently.

2. Transfer the antipasto to the bread bowl, sprinkle with Parmesan cheese, and serve with the remaining dressing on the side.

SIZZLINGBEEFFAJITASALAD

A base of fresh spinach wilts under a blanket of sautéed vegetables and sizzling marinated steak in this sensational salad. The hearty sourdough bread partners perfectly with the spicy fajita filling.

1. In a large bowl, whisk together all of the marinade ingredients. Add the steak and turn to coat. Cover and refrigerate at least 2 hours, turning the steak occasionally as it marinates.

2. Preheat the broiler.

3. Heat the oil in a large skillet over high heat. Add the bell peppers, onion, and garlic, reduce the heat to low, and sauté the mixture about 7 minutes, or until the peppers and onions are soft. Turn off the heat.

4. Broil the steak about four inches from the heat source for 5 minutes on each side, or until fully cooked. Transfer the meat to a cutting board and let stand for 10 minutes before thinly slicing.

5. Add the meat to the skillet with the sautéed vegetables, and heat for a minute or until the mixture sizzles.

6. Place the spinach in the bottom of the bread bowl, top with the sizzling fajita mixture, and serve.

YIELD: 4 SERVINGS

1 ½ pounds skirt steak

2 tablespoons vegetable oil

1 ½ cups thinly sliced red bell peppers

1 ½ cups thinly sliced green bell peppers

½ cup thinly sliced red onion

2 garlic cloves, minced

3 cups fresh spinach, torn into large bite-sized pieces

1- to 1 ¾-pound bread bowl

MARINADE

4 garlic cloves, minced

¼ cup fresh lime juice

2 tablespoons olive oil

1 teaspoon ground cumin

1 teaspoon chile powder

1 teaspoon ground coriander

1 teaspoon black pepper

¼ teaspoon salt

SCOMA'S-INSPIRED WARM**CIOPPINO**SALAD

Our friend Steve Scarabosio, longtime executive chef at legendary Scoma's on San Francisco's Fisherman's Wharf, is a maestro when it comes to making the delicious seafood stew called "cioppino." His popular stew served as our inspiration for this warm cioppino salad.

YIELD: 4 SERVINGS

1 tablespoon plus
1 ½ teaspoons olive oil

1 clove garlic, minced

½ cup chopped onions

½ cup red wine

1 teaspoon chopped
fresh oregano

1 ½ teaspoons chopped
fresh basil

3 cups tomato sauce

4 ounces rock cod,
cut into 1-inch cubes

4 ounces clams
(without shells)

4 ounces prawns

4 ounces sea scallops

¾ cup fish stock or clam juice

4 ounces crabmeat,
or whole cooked crab,
cleaned and cracked

1. Heat 1 tablespoon of the olive oil in a large pot over medium-low heat. Add the garlic and sauté 1 minute, then toss in the onions, and continue to sauté 2 minutes. Stir the wine into the pot along with the oregano and basil, and continue to cook until the liquid is reduced by half.

2. Add the tomato sauce, cod, clams, prawns, and scallops. Increase the heat and bring the ingredients to a boil. Reduce the heat to low and simmer for 3 to 5 minutes.

3. Add the fish stock, crabmeat, and shrimp. Simmer 1 minute and add the salt and pepper. Remove the pot from the heat and set aside. (At this point, you can spoon this hot cioppino into a bread bowl and serve it as a stew.)

4. Preheat the oven to 350°F.

5. Heat the remaining 1½ teaspoons of olive oil in a small skillet over low heat. Add the spinach and sauté for 1 minute, or until just wilted.

6. Warm the bread bowl in the oven for 2 to 3 minutes. Carefully remove the warm bowl, and add the spinach. Reserving the broth, drain the hot cioppino and add it to the bread bowl. Drizzle with 3 tablespoons of the reserved broth.

7. Serve the warm salad with the remaining broth on the side. Save any unused broth for another recipe.

4 ounces medium-sized shrimp, shelled and deveined

Salt, to taste

Black pepper, to taste

1 1/2 cups fresh spinach, torn into bite-sized pieces

1- to 1 3/4-pound bread bowl

What's a Prawn?

Resembling tiny Maine lobsters (about 6 inches in length), prawns—also called langostino, langoustine, Danish lobsters, Italian scampi, Dublin Bay prawns, and Florida lobsterettes—are members of the lobster family. The meat of these crustaceans is sweet, delicate, and reminiscent of lobster. Be aware that some seafood sellers and restaurants incorrectly call jumbo shrimp "prawns."

WARM COBB SALAD

Warm bacon and melted blue cheese crown
our bread bowl version of the classic Cobb salad.

½ head iceberg lettuce, torn into bite-sized pieces

1 cup ranch dressing

3 hard boiled eggs, chopped

1 avocado, peeled and diced

2 tomatoes, seeded and chopped

2 cups chopped cooked chicken breast

¾ cup crumbled blue cheese

6 slices cooked bacon, cut into ½-inch squares

1- to 1¾-pound bread bowl

1. Preheat the broiler.

2. Place the lettuce in the bread bowl and drizzle with 1 table-spoon of the dressing.

3. Add the eggs, avocado, tomatoes, and chicken. Drizzle with 1½ tablespoons of dressing.

4. Sprinkle the blue cheese and bacon on top. Wrap the bowl with aluminum foil, leaving the top uncovered. Place under the broiler for 1 minute, or until the bacon is heated and the cheese begins to melt.

5. Carefully remove the foil, and serve the salad with the remaining dressing on the side.

6.Soup'sOn!

Nothing is more reminiscent of the restaurants on Fisherman's Wharf than New England-style clam chowder served in a crisp sourdough bread bowl. Thousands of tourists visit the San Francisco landmark each year just for a taste of this legendary dish. The good news is that the legend doesn't have to end with clam chowder—many soups are absolutely wonderful when served in edible sourdough bread bowls.

We kick off this chapter with our delectable version of the famous clam chowder that started it all, and then continue with an exciting repertoire of soups that pair perfectly with sourdough bread bowls. You'll find recipes such as Francesca's Seafood Chowder—an outstanding combination of shrimp, scallops, and prawns in a thick, creamy bacon-flavored base—as well as hot and hearty favorites like Broccoli Cheese Soup and Minted Fresh Pea. For a soup that eats like a meal, nothing satisfies like our Chicken and Dumplings; and cheese lovers will flip over our tantalizing Blue Cheese Soup—a buttery blend that perfectly complements the crunchy goodness of sourdough bread. If you are a fan of onion soup, don't pass up the Wine Country Onion Soup with its crown of melted pepperjack cheese.

When using your own favorite recipes, keep in mind that thick soups are recommended. All of our recipes are formulated to fit into 1- to 1³/₄-pound bowls, but you can serve them in smaller, individual-sized bread bowls as well. One thing is certain, whether you're serving the soup from a large bread bowl or enjoying it directly from individual containers, you're going to love the recipe choices in this chapter. Enjoy!

FISHERMAN'SWHARF-STYLECLAMCHOWDER

*Our version of this time-honored chowder is garnished
with a sprinkling of crisped salt pork, which lends
a delicious touch to the creamy classic.*

YIELD: 6 SERVINGS

2 tablespoons diced
salt pork, or 1 strip bacon

1 medium yellow onion,
finely chopped

1 stalk celery, diced

2 tablespoons
all-purpose flour

2 cups clam juice

1 medium potato,
peeled and diced

1/4 teaspoon dried thyme

1 cup fresh or canned
chopped clams

1 cup heavy cream

Salt, to taste

Black pepper, to taste

2 drops Tabasco sauce

1- to 1 3/4-pound bread bowl

1. Place the salt pork in a medium pot over medium heat. While stirring, cook the pork for 2 minutes or until crisp. Transfer to a plate and set aside.

2. Without cleaning the pot, add the onion and celery. Sauté over medium-low heat for 5 minutes, or until the onions are translucent and the celery begins to soften.

3. Sprinkle the flour over the onion-celery mixture, and stir to form a paste. Add the clam juice, potato, and thyme. Increase the heat and bring the ingredients to a boil. Reduce the heat to low, and simmer covered for 15 minutes, or until the potatoes are tender.

4. Add the clams to the pot, and stir in the cream. Continue to simmer (do not allow the mixture to boil) for 5 minutes, or thick and creamy. Add the salt, pepper, and Tabasco sauce.

5. Spoon the chowder into the bread bowl, garnish with salt pork, and serve.

FRANCESCA'S**SEAFOOD**CHOWDER

*John's wife, Francesca, created this superb seafood chowder—
an outstanding combination of scallops, shrimp, and prawns
in a creamy sauce with the subtle flavor of smoky bacon.
Her chowder has become a favorite among many of
John's friends who are award-winning chefs.*

YIELD: 6 SERVINGS

1 pound sea scallops

8 ounces prawns*

8 ounces medium shrimp,
shelled and deveined

8 ounces sliced bacon

1 small onion, chopped

12-ounce package frozen
hash browns with
onions and peppers

4 cups half-and-half

4 cups milk

¼ cup all-purpose flour

1- to 1¾-pound
bread bowl

1. Place the scallops and prawns in a large stockpot over high heat with enough water to cover, and bring to a boil. Reduce the heat to low and simmer for 10 minutes. Add the shrimp and continue to simmer 2 minutes or until the seafood is cooked. Turn off the heat.

2. In a large skillet, cook the bacon until crisp. Transfer to paper towels and let cool. Crumble and set aside.

3. Without cleaning the skillet, add the onion and frozen hash browns. Sauté over medium-low heat for 5 minutes, or until the onions are soft and the potatoes are heated through. Transfer to the pot with the seafood mixture, and return the heat to medium. Stir in the half-and-half and milk.

4. Ladle a cup or two of liquid from the pot into a small bowl, add the flour, and stir or whisk until smooth. Stir the flour mixture back into the pot, continuing to stir about 3 minutes, or until the chowder heats and thickens.

5. Spoon the chowder into the bread bowl, garnish with bacon, and serve.

* See "What's a Prawn" on page 61.

CORN'N'CRAB CHOWDER

*This thick, delicious chowder gets
a flavorful jolt from bacon and beer!*

YIELD: **4** SERVINGS

4 tablespoons unsalted butter

I small onion, chopped

I teaspoon dried thyme

1/4 cup green bell pepper,
chopped

1/4 cup red bell pepper,
chopped

3/4 cup beer or ale

1/2 cup all-purpose flour

1 1/2 cups warm milk

3/4 cup corn kernels

1/2 cup sour cream

1/2 cup crabmeat

1/2 cup corn chips, slightly
crumbled for garnish

2 crumbled bacon strips,
for garnish

1- to 1 3/4-pound bread bowl

1. Melt 1 tablespoon of the butter in a medium stockpot over medium-low heat. Add the onion, and sauté for 3 minutes, or until soft and translucent. Add the thyme and bell peppers, and cook another 3 minutes, or until the peppers are soft. Stir in the beer, reduce the heat to low, and simmer 15 minutes.

2. Melt the remaining butter in a medium skillet set over medium-low heat. Sprinkle the flour over the butter, and stir to mix well. Continue to cook, stirring gently, until light beige in color. Slowly stir in the milk, then add this mixture to the stockpot with the simmering bell-pepper mixture.

3. Add the corn to the stockpot, increase the heat to medium-low, and cook while stirring for 10 minutes, or until the chowder has thickened.

4. Spoon the hot chowder into the bread bowl. Stir in the sour cream and crabmeat, sprinkle with corn chips and bacon, and serve.

WINECOUNTRY**ONION**SOUP

*Although traditional French onion soup calls for brandy or
French wine, we "California-ize" ours with a good California
Chardonnay. To complete its West Coast influence and appeal,
we choose Monterey pepperjack cheese to melt on top.*

1. Preheat the broiler.

2. Melt the butter in a large stockpot over medium heat, and add the onions and sugar. Stirring often, cook for 10 to 15 minutes, or until the onions are soft and beginning to brown.

3. Sprinkle the flour and salt over the onions, and stir until well mixed. While stirring, slowly add the broth and Chardonnay, increase the heat, and bring to a boil. Reduce the heat to low, cover and simmer, stirring occasionally, for 12 minutes, or until the broth thickens a bit.

4. Spoon the soup into the bread bowl. Tuck the sourdough slices just under the surface of the soup and top with the cheese.

5. Wrap the bowl with aluminum foil, leaving the top uncovered. Place the bowl under the broiler about 3 minutes, or until the cheese melts. Carefully remove the foil before serving.

YIELD: 6 SERVINGS

4 tablespoons butter

5 large onions, sliced

3 teaspoons sugar

$1/4$ cup all-purpose flour

$1/2$ teaspoon salt

8 cups beef broth

1 cup California Chardonnay

2 slices sourdough bread

4 thick slices Monterey pepperjack cheese

1- to $1^3/4$-pound bread bowl

BROCCOLICHEDDARSOUP

*This show-stopping soup, rich with melted
Cheddar cheese and sweet broccoli, is an excellent
choice when having guests for dinner.*

YIELD: 6 SERVINGS

6 cups water

10-ounce package frozen
chopped broccoli

$1/2$ cup chopped onion

1 $1/2$ teaspoons salt

1 teaspoon garlic powder

$1/2$ teaspoon black pepper

2 cups shredded mild
Cheddar cheese

1 cup half-and-half

1 cup milk

$1/4$ cup butter

$1/3$ cup all-purpose flour

Shredded Cheddar cheese
for garnish

1- to 1$3/4$-pound bread bowl

1. Bring the water to boil in a large stockpot over medium-high heat. Add the broccoli and onion, cook for 10 minutes, then add the salt, garlic powder, and pepper.

2. Add the cheese to the pot and stir until melted. While stirring, add the half-and-half, milk, and butter. Continue to stir until the mixture almost returns to a boil, then remove from the heat.

3. In a small bowl whisk or stir the flour with $1/2$ cup cold water until smooth. Stir the flour mixture into the pot. Return the heat to medium and stir continuously until the soup thickens.

4. Spoon the hot soup into the bread bowl, garnish with Cheddar cheese, and serve.

MINTEDFRESHPEASOUP

A flavorful blend of fresh peas, split peas, and zucchini are enhanced by a kiss of mint in this light refreshing soup that is delicious served hot or cold.

YIELD: 6 SERVINGS

1. Place the split peas and water in a large stockpot over medium heat. Cook about 30 minutes, or until the peas are tender. Add the fresh peas and zucchini, and continue to cook another 10 minutes.

2. Carefully transfer the mixture to a blender or food processor along with the mint, salt, pepper, and curry. Purée until smooth. (You can do this in two or three batches.)

3. Return the mixture to the pot and heat, or, if cold soup is preferred, refrigerate until chilled. Spoon the soup into the bread bowl and serve.

³/₄ cup dried split peas

3 cups water

2 cups fresh peas, or frozen and thawed

¹/₂ cup peeled, cubed zucchini

3 tablespoons fresh chopped mint

¹/₂ teaspoon salt

¹/₄ teaspoon black pepper

¹/₄ teaspoon curry powder

1- to 1 ³/₄-pound bread bowl

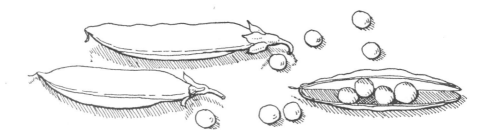

BRANDIED YAM SOUP

*Rich, nutritious, and satisfyingly sweet, this luscious
gourmet soup has the added crunch of candied
pecans and a mini-marshmallow garnish.*

YIELD: 6 SERVINGS

2 cans yams in light syrup
(1 pound 13 ounces each),
drained

1 cup chicken broth

4 cups half-and-half

1/4 cup brandy or maple syrup

1/4 teaspoon nutmeg

1/4 teaspoon cinnamon

2 heaping tablespoons
chopped candied pecans
(see page 53)

Handful miniature
marshmallows

1- to 1 3/4-pound bread bowl

1. Place the yams in a blender or food processor, and blend until creamy. Add the broth and continue to blend until well combined.

2. Transfer the mixture to a large saucepan and bring to a boil. While stirring, add the half-and-half, brandy, nutmeg, and cinnamon. Reduce the heat to low and simmer about 15 minutes.

3. Spoon the soup into the bread bowl, top with pecans and marshmallows, and serve.

MINESTRONETHAT'S**A**MEAL

In Tuscany, this soup is traditionally served in a tureen between layers of day-old bread. We serve it the same way, only our tureen is a crusty bread bowl.

YIELD: 4 SERVINGS

1 ½ tablespoons olive oil

2 cloves garlic, chopped

¾ cup chopped red onion

1 carrot, sliced

1 stalk celery, chopped

2 cups chicken broth

1 large peeled potato, cubed

3 medium tomatoes, seeded and chopped

½ cup fresh or frozen peas

⅓ cup bite-sized pieces cooked chicken

⅓ cup bite-sized pieces cooked Italian sausage

2 tablespoons dried parsley

¼ teaspoon dried rosemary

¼ teaspoon dried thyme

1 cup cooked cannellini beans

6 medium shrimp, cooked

¼ teaspoon salt

¼ teaspoon black pepper

2 slices day-old sourdough bread

Grated Parmesan cheese for garnish

1- to 1¾-pound bread bowl

1. Heat the oil in a large stockpot over medium heat. Add the garlic, onion, carrot, and celery. Sauté about 5 minutes, or until the ingredients are soft. Reduce the heat to medium-low, and add the broth, potatoes, tomatoes, peas, chicken, sausage, parsley, rosemary, and thyme. Simmer about 15 minutes, or until the potatoes are soft.

2. Using a fork, mash half the beans and add them to the soup along with the remaining whole beans and the shrimp. Simmer another 5 minutes. Add the salt and pepper.

3. Ladle a third of the soup into the bread bowl and top with a slice of sourdough bread. Top with another third of the soup, add the other slice of bread, and finish with the remaining soup and a sprinkling of Parmesan. Serve with more Parmesan on the side.

4. To enjoy any leftovers as a next-day casserole, wrap the bowl with the leftover soup in aluminum foil and refrigerate. Before serving, uncover and sprinkle with 1 or 2 teaspoons olive oil and some Parmesan cheese. Rewrap completely and bake in a preheated 350°F oven for 25 minutes, or until piping hot. Cut into wedges and serve.

CHICKENANDDUMPLINGS

*This heartwarming soup with old-fashioned
chicken and dumplings is stick-to-the-ribs good!
Great to serve on cold-weather days.*

YIELD: 6 SERVINGS

1 whole chicken
(about 2 1/2 pounds)

5 cups water

3 cups chicken broth

2 carrots, coarsely chopped

1 medium yellow onion,
coarsely chopped

2 stalks celery, coarsely
chopped

1 teaspoon salt

1 teaspoon black pepper

1- to 1 3/4-pound bread bowl

DUMPLINGS

2 cups all-purpose flour

1/2 teaspoon baking powder

1/2 teaspoon salt

3 tablespoons shortening

1 cup milk

1. Place all of the soup ingredients in a large stockpot over high heat and bring to a boil. Reduce the heat to low, cover, and simmer 60 minutes.

2. Remove the chicken from the pot and place on a large platter to cool.

3. When the chicken is cool enough to handle, remove the meat from the bones and return it to the pot of simmering broth.

4. To prepare the dumplings, combine the flour, baking powder, and salt in a large bowl. Cut in the shortening and add the milk, a little at a time, stirring until the ingredients form a moist dough.

5. Turn the dough onto a floured surface and knead five or six times. Scoop generous portions of the dough with a tablespoon, and drop them carefully into the simmering soup. (Do not let the broth boil.) Cover the pot and simmer the dumplings 7 to 10 minutes, or until they become plump and a wooden toothpick inserted into the center comes out clean.

6. Spoon the soup into the bread bowl and serve.

BLUE**CHEESE**SOUP

"Decadent"—a great word for describing this rich
and buttery blue cheese soup, which partners perfectly
with its sourdough surroundings.

YIELD: 6 SERVINGS

1. Melt the butter in a large stockpot over medium heat. Add the carrots, celery, and onion, and cook about 8 minutes, or until the onions are golden brown.

2. Add the stock, cream, and cauliflower. Cook about 5 minutes, or until the cauliflower is tender. Add the blue cheese and reduce the heat to low. Simmer about 3 minutes, or until the cheese is melted.

3. Carefully transfer the mixture to a blender or food processor, and purée until smooth. (You can do this in two or three batches.)

4. Return the puréed mixture to the pot and heat. Spoon the hot soup into the bread bowl, garnish with pepper, and serve.

4 tablespoons butter

2 carrots, diced

2 stalks celery, diced

1 medium yellow onion, chopped

4 cups beef stock

1 cup cream

1 small head cauliflower (about 1 pound), cut into small pieces

1 cup crumbled blue cheese (Roquefort, Stilton, Gorgonzola, or a combination of)

Black pepper for garnish

1- to 1 3/4-pound bread bowl

Preparing Roux

A mixture of flour and fat (usually butter) in equal proportions, roux is used as a thickener for sauces, soups, and stews. The recipe below yields enough roux to thicken a half gallon of liquid.

YIELD: ABOUT 1 CUP

1 cup butter
1 cup unbleached white flour

1. Melt the butter in a heavy skillet over very low heat (be careful not to burn). Sprinkle the flour a little at a time over the melted butter, stirring constantly for 1 minute, or until the mixture is thick, smooth, and turns a pale beige color. Remove from the heat and allow to cool. (For darker roux, cook a little longer—stirring constantly to prevent burning—until the desired color is reached.)

2. Place the roux in a covered container and store in the refrigerator, where it will keep for two or three weeks.

CHEF JAY VEREGGE'S SHRIMP, PRAWN, AND LOBSTER BISQUE

This incredible bisque is a testament to the culinary creativity of Chef Jay Veregge, formerly of San Francisco's famous Tadich Grill. Fresh pears, cream sherry, and a touch of vanilla are just a few of the ingredients that give this bisque its indescribable flavor.

YIELD: 8 SERVINGS

2 tablespoons vegetable oil

I medium yellow onion, diced

I cup diced celery

I bay leaf

I pound shrimp shells

8 cups fish or vegetable stock

I $\frac{1}{2}$ teaspoons vanilla extract

2 pears, peeled and sliced, or I cup canned peaches

$\frac{1}{4}$ cup tomato paste

Meat of I $\frac{1}{2}$-pound lobster

$\frac{3}{4}$ cup roux (see page 74)

I cup heavy cream

I cup cream sherry

$\frac{1}{2}$ cup fresh lemon juice

8 ounces shrimp, shelled, deveined, and finely chopped

8 ounces medium prawns*

Chopped chives for garnish

2 bread bowls (I- to I$\frac{3}{4}$-pounds each)

1. Place the oil, onion, celery, bay leaf, and shrimp shells in a large stockpot over low heat, and sauté 10 to 12 minutes. Add the stock, vanilla, pears, and tomato paste. Increase the heat to medium, cover, and let the ingredients boil for 1 hour.

2. Strain the broth until it is clear. Add the lobster, reduce the heat to low, and simmer for 30 minutes. Increase the heat to medium, and slowly add the roux, stirring constantly until the broth comes to a boil. Add the cream, sherry, lemon juice, shrimp, and prawns, continuing to stir until the bisque is smooth and creamy.

3. Ladle the bisque into the bread bowls, garnish with chives, and serve.

* See "What's a Prawn" on page 61

CREAMYPEANUTSOUP

YIELD: 6 SERVINGS

3 cups chicken broth

1 cup creamy peanut butter

½ teaspoon salt, or to taste

1 cup cream

½ cup milk

Chopped peanuts for garnish

1- to 1¾-pound bread bowl

*Housed in a bread bowl, this creamy (and we do mean "creamy")
soup is reminiscent of a gourmet peanut butter sandwich.*

1. Bring the broth to a boil in a medium saucepan over
medium heat. Add the peanut butter and salt, stirring until
smooth and well blended.

2. Stir in the cream and milk. Heat for a minute or so, but do
not let boil.

3. Pour the soup into the bread bowl,
garnish with peanuts,
and serve.

7.Savory**Stews**

ccording to its most basic definition, a stew is the combination of two or more foods—usually fish, meat, and/or vegetables—that are slow-simmered in a flavorful broth. Inexpensive, tougher cuts of meat typically work well in this type of dish as the slow-simmering process acts as a tenderizer. Thick, hearty, and satisfying, stews are characteristically considered "comfort" foods—perfect to serve in sourdough bread bowls.

This chapter includes a number of outstanding recipes, both traditional and innovative. Flavorful lamb has always been a favorite stew ingredient choice, and our savory Garlic Lamb Stew, complete with hearty vegetables and sourdough bread "dumplings," will not disappoint. The Greek-inspired Stefatho, direct from John's family recipe files, is a heartwarming combination of braised beef and onions in a tantalizing tomato-based sauce.

Northern California's wine country served as the inspiration for our California Wine and Cheese Stew—a fondue-like mélange of melted cheese, potato chunks, and shredded chicken in a buttery, white wine sauce. And the Very, Very, Very Good Vegetable Stew, flavored with sherry and brown sugar, is always a hit among vegetarians and nonvegetarians alike. One taste of our Popcorn Shrimp Gumbo will transport you to Bourbon Street in New Orleans, while the Hot Italian Sausage Stew and the Hearty Chicken with Basil will place you under the Tuscan sun.

Once you've tried some of the stews on the following pages, you'll understand why they are among our favorites. We're guessing they will become some of yours as well.

GARLICLAMBSTEWWITH BREADBOWLDUMPLINGS

*Be sure to choose lean cuts of lamb for this hot, hearty,
and satisfyingly delicious stew, and use the bread from
the hollowed-out bowl to form the "dumplings."*

YIELD: 4 SERVINGS

1 tablespoon olive oil

1 pound lean lamb stew meat, or bite-sized pieces from the leg or shoulder (trimmed of any fat)

1 small onion, chopped

2 carrots, cut into bite-sized pieces

1 stalk celery, cut into bite-sized pieces

5 cloves garlic, sliced

1 teaspoon chopped Italian parsley

$\frac{1}{2}$ teaspoon thyme

3 cups beef broth

1 pound small red potatoes, cut into bite-sized pieces

Salt, to taste

Black pepper, to taste

Bread from the hollowed-out bowl

1- to 1$\frac{3}{4}$-pound bread bowl

1. Heat the oil in a large heavy-bottomed pot over medium heat. Add the lamb and brown on all sides. Add the onion, carrots, and celery, and cook about 5 minutes, or until the onions are translucent. Add the garlic, parsley, thyme, and broth.

2. Bring the ingredients to a boil, then reduce the heat to low. Cover and simmer 1 hour.

3. Add the potatoes and continue to simmer 30 minutes, or until the potatoes are tender. Add the salt and pepper.

4. While the potatoes simmer, squeeze chunks of the sourdough bread with your hand to form 8 "dumplings." Add them to the pot during the last 3 minutes of simmering.

5. Spoon the stew into the bread bowl and serve.

STEFATHO

Another Greek dish from John's family recipe files, Stefatho is a hearty braised beef and onion stew flavored with an interesting blend of cinnamon, allspice, and cloves.

YIELD: 4 SERVINGS

1/4 cup olive oil

1 1/2 pounds chuck, cut into 2-inch cubes

1 clove garlic, minced

2 cups water

6-ounce can tomato paste

3 cloves garlic, whole

1 cinnamon stick

2 cloves

3 tablespoons vinegar

2 tablespoons red wine

2 tablespoons sugar

1 teaspoon salt

1/4 teaspoon allspice

Black pepper, to taste

1 small onion, minced

1- to 1 3/4-pound bread bowl

1. Heat the oil in a large heavy-bottomed pot over medium heat. Add the beef and minced garlic, and brown the beef on all sides. Add all of the remaining ingredients except the onion, and stir until well blended.

2. Bring the ingredients to a boil, then reduce heat, cover, and allow to simmer 1 1/2 hours.

3. Add the onion and continue to simmer an additional 30 minutes, or until the beef is tender. With a slotted spoon, remove and discard the garlic cloves, cinnamon stick, and cloves.

4. Spoon the stew into the bread bowl and serve.

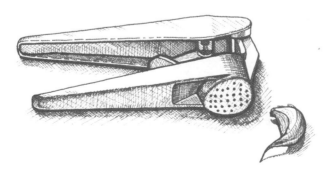

SPICY**SOUTHWESTERN** **GROUND**BEEF**STEW**

Some people call this dish a stew, others call it chili.
We just call it easy. For those who like it really hot, add a
few extra dashes of Tabasco sauce and/or additional chiles.

YIELD: 4 SERVINGS

I pound lean ground beef

I small onion, coarsely chopped

I clove garlic, minced

³/₄ cup finely chopped fresh jalapeño chiles*

¹/₄ teaspoon Tabasco sauce, or to taste

14.5-ounce can whole stewed tomatoes, coarsely chopped

I cup water

I cup fresh corn kernels, or frozen and thawed

Salt, to taste

Black pepper, to taste

1- to 1³/₄-pound bread bowl

---

*When preparing the peppers, be sure to wear gloves, and be careful not to touch your eyes.

1. Brown the beef in a large heavy-bottomed pot over medium heat. Drain the excess fat. Add the onion, garlic, chiles, and Tabasco sauce, and mix with the beef. Stir in the tomatoes, water, corn, salt, and pepper. Reduce the heat to low, cover, and simmer for 1 hour.

2. Spoon the stew into the bread bowl and serve.

HOTITALIANSAUSAGESTEW

It was in a little out-of-the-way gourmet shop in the San Francisco Bay Area, where John found the fig balsamic vinegar he uses in this stew. Its tangy yet smooth flavor is an excellent addition, although any good balsamic vinegar works well.

YIELD: 4 SERVINGS

1 tablespoon plus 1 teaspoon olive oil

8 ounces hot Italian sausage

1 medium onion, chopped

1/2 cup water

2 tablespoons balsamic vinegar (preferably fruit flavored)

3 carrots, cut into large bite-sized pieces

3 medium red potatoes, cut into large bite-sized pieces

1 1/2 cups diced ripe tomatoes

1 large clove garlic, minced

1 teaspoon chopped fresh thyme

1 teaspoon chopped fresh rosemary

Salt, to taste

Black pepper, to taste

Finely chopped parsley for garnish

1- to 1 3/4-pound bread bowl

1. Heat 1 tablespoon of the oil in a large heavy-bottomed pot over medium heat, add the sausage, and brown on all sides. Transfer the sausage to a cutting board, and cut into large bite-sized pieces.

2. Add the remaining teaspoon of oil to the pot along with the onion and sausage pieces. Cook over medium heat about 7 minutes, or until the onion is translucent. Add the water, vinegar, carrots, potatoes, tomatoes, garlic, thyme, and rosemary, and stir well.

3. Bring the ingredients to a boil, then reduce the heat to low. Cover the pot and simmer for 45 minutes, stirring occasionally, until the potatoes are tender. Add the salt and pepper. (If the stew is too thick, add a little water to reach the desired consistency.)

4. Spoon the stew into the bread bowl, sprinkle with parsley, and serve.

POPCORNSHRIMP**GUMBO**

We've added crisp, cayenne-flavored popcorn shrimp to andouille sausage and crabmeat in this Creole-seasoned New Orleans-style gumbo. When eaten along with pieces of the bread bowl, it's like a Po'Boy Sandwich—another New Orleans' staple.

YIELD: 4 SERVINGS

8 ounces andouille sausage, cut into bite-sized pieces

1/4 cup vegetable oil

1/4 cup all-purpose flour

5 cups seafood or vegetable broth

1 tablespoon butter or margarine

1 medium onion, chopped

3/4 cup cut fresh, canned, or frozen okra

3 cloves garlic, chopped

1/4 cup flat-leaf parsley, chopped

3 stalks celery, chopped

3 scallions, including green parts, chopped

3/4 cup chopped green pepper

12 ounces cooked medium shrimp

4 ounces crabmeat

1 teaspoon seasoned salt

Black pepper, to taste

1 1/2 tablespoons Creole seasoning

1- to 1 3/4-pound bread bowl

1. In a medium skillet, brown the sausage over medium heat, then transfer to paper towels. Drain the excess fat from the skillet and set aside.

2. Heat the oil in a large heavy-bottomed pot over medium heat. Slowly add the flour while stirring constantly until caramel colored, then add 2 cups of the broth, continuing to stir until well blended. Add the remaining broth and reduce the heat to very low. Stirring occasionally, simmer for 5 minutes or until the broth begins to thicken.

3. While the broth simmers, melt the margarine in the same skillet used to cook the sausage over medium-low heat. Add the onion, okra, garlic, parsley, celery, scallions, and bell pepper, and cook for 5 minutes, or until the ingredients just begin to soften. Transfer to the pot with the simmering broth, cover, and continue to cook for 45 minutes.

4. While the gumbo is cooking, prepare the shrimp. Preheat the broiler. Coat a baking sheet with cooking spray and set aside. Combine the breadcrumbs and tarragon in a pie plate or large dish. In a medium bowl, combine the remaining coating ingredients.

5. Coat the shrimp with the mayonnaise mixture, then dredge in the breadcrumbs to completely cover. Place the shrimp on the baking sheet and place under the broiler for 2 minutes. Carefully turn and broil 2 more minutes until golden brown. Remove and set aside.

6. Add the sausage and crabmeat to the gumbo, reduce the heat to very low, and cook an additional 10 minutes. Add the seasoned salt, salt, and pepper. Remove from the heat and stir in the Creole seasoning.

7. Spoon the gumbo into the bread bowl. Gently tuck the shrimp just under the surface of the stew. Serve hot.

SHRIMP COATING

$1/2$ cup breadcrumbs*

$1/2$ teaspoon dried tarragon

$1/4$ cup mayonnaise

2 tablespoons Dijon mustard

1 tablespoon lemon juice

1 tablespoon chopped parsley

2 dashes Tabasco sauce

1 teaspoon cayenne pepper

1 teaspoon chile powder

1 teaspoon ground cumin

$1/4$ teaspoon salt

---

*To make breadcrumbs from the hollowed-out bowl, see page 13.

HEARTY CHICKEN STEW WITH BASIL

The addition of fresh basil and garbanzo beans gives this traditional chicken stew a flavorful new dimension that will have you clamoring for more.

YIELD: 4 SERVINGS

1 tablespoon olive oil

1 stalk celery, chopped

1 small green bell pepper, chopped

1 medium carrot, peeled and chopped

1 small onion, chopped

1 cup chicken broth

2 large tomatoes (about 8 ounces), chopped

$\frac{1}{2}$ cup tomato puree

Pinch dried rosemary

2 pounds chicken thighs and breasts (with bones)

$\frac{3}{4}$ cup cooked garbanzo beans, rinsed and drained

$\frac{1}{2}$ cup fresh basil leaves

Salt, to taste

Black pepper, to taste

1- to 1$\frac{3}{4}$-pound bread bowl

1. Heat the oil in a large heavy-bottomed pot over medium heat. Add the celery, bell pepper, carrot, and onion, and cook about 5 minutes, or until the onion is translucent.

2. Add the broth, tomatoes, tomato puree, and rosemary to the pot, and stir well. Add the chicken.

3. Increase the heat and bring the ingredients to a boil. Reduce the heat to medium-low, cover, and simmer about 40 minutes, or until the chicken is fully cooked and tender. Remove the chicken and place on a large plate to cool. Add the garbanzo beans to the pot.

4. When the chicken is cool enough to handle, remove the meat from the bones and return it to the pot. Tear the basil leaves and stir them into the stew along with the salt and pepper.

5. Spoon the stew into the bread bowl and serve.

VERY,**VERY,**VERY**GOOD** **VEGETABLE**STEW

Vegetarians and nonvegetarians alike will flip for this show-stopping stew. Its extensive cast of ingredients is spotlighted in a rich, spicy sauce that is sure to garner rave reviews.

1. Heat the oil in a large heavy-bottomed pot over medium-low heat. Add the onion, celery, carrot, and bell pepper, and sauté for 5 minutes, or until soft but not brown.

2. Add all of the remaining ingredients, increase the heat, and bring to a boil. Reduce the heat to medium-low, and simmer for 30 minutes.

3. Spoon the stew into the bread bowl and serve.

YIELD: 4 SERVINGS

1 ½ teaspoons olive oil

1 cup chopped onion

1 stalk celery, chopped

1 carrot, chopped

1 small red bell pepper, chopped

2 cups cooked black beans

1 cup vegetable broth

1 cup fresh corn kernels, or frozen and thawed

1 medium tomato, diced

1 clove garlic, chopped

3 tablespoons dry sherry

1 tablespoon tomato paste

¼ cup chopped fresh cilantro

1 tablespoon chile powder

1 tablespoon brown sugar

1 teaspoon ground cumin

Pinch dried oregano

1- to 1 ¾-pound bread bowl

CHEF**CLYDE**SERDA'S
GREENCHILE**AND**PORK
COUNTRYSTEW

YIELD: 4 SERVINGS

4 green Anaheim
chile peppers

1 jalapeño pepper

1 tablespoon vegetable oil

1 1/2 pounds cubed pork
stew meat, or meat from
pork chops (if using chops,
after removing the meat,
reserve the bones to
cook in the sauce)

1 small onion, finely diced

2 cloves garlic, minced

4 cups water

2 medium potatoes
(preferably Yukon gold),
peeled and cut into
1/2-inch cubes

2 ripe tomatoes
(preferably Roma), quartered

1 1/2 teaspoons dried oregano

1 1/2 teaspoons ground cumin

1/2 teaspoon ground
coriander

Salt, to taste

*Award-winning Chef Clyde Serda, longtime instructor at the California
Culinary Academy in San Francisco, has been featured on their PBS
TV series as well as in their best-selling cookbooks. He has chosen this
stew (which he serves in a bread bowl) as his all-time favorite recipe!
Shredded bread from the hollowed-out bowl is used as a thickener.*

1. To roast the Anaheim and jalapeño chiles,* first heat a skillet over medium heat. Cut a small slit in each pepper and
place them in the hot skillet. Turn the peppers as they blister and char. When completely charred, immediately wrap
them in a clean, moist kitchen towel and let cool (this will
help loosen their skin). Peel off the skin, slit the chiles with
a knife, and remove the seeds. Chop and set aside.

2. Heat the oil in a large heavy-bottomed pot over medium-
low heat. Add the pork (and bones if using) and brown the
meat. Add the onion and garlic, and sauté about 5 minutes,
or until the onion is translucent.

3. Add the water, and stir to deglaze the bottom of the pot.
Add the potatoes, increase the heat, and bring to a boil.
Reduce the heat to low and simmer for 15 minutes.

---

* When preparing the peppers, be sure to wear gloves, and be careful not to
touch your eyes.

4. Stir the roasted chiles into the pot, along with the tomatoes, oregano, cumin, and coriander. Add the salt and adjust the seasonings. Cover the pot and simmer for 20 minutes, or until the potatoes are tender.

5. Using a slotted spoon, remove any bones from the pot. Stir in the bread and cilantro.

6. Spoon the stew into the bread bowl, sprinkle with cheese, and serve.

$\frac{1}{2}$ cup shredded bread from the hollowed-out bowl

$\frac{1}{2}$ cup coarsely chopped fresh cilantro,

$\frac{3}{4}$ cup shredded Monterey pepperjack cheese, or plain Monterey Jack

1- to 1 $\frac{3}{4}$-pound bread bowl

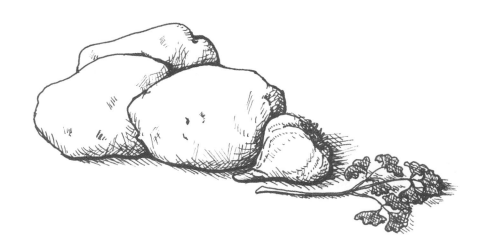

CALIFORNIAWINEAND CHEESESTEW

YIELD: 6 SERVINGS

1 ½ pounds assorted cheese varieties, cut into ½-inch cubes*

½ cup white wine

4 tablespoons softened unsalted butter

1 clove garlic, minced

1 tablespoon chopped fresh tarragon

1 tablespoon chopped fresh marjoram

1 tablespoon chopped fresh basil

1 ½ cups shredded cooked chicken

3 small cooked red potatoes, cut into bite-sized pieces

1- to 1 ¾-pound bread bowl

When the party's over and you find yourself with an assortment of leftover cheeses, try this French-inspired fondue-like creation. It is the perfect filling for a crisp sourdough bread bowl.

1. In a food processor, combine all of the ingredients except the chicken and potatoes, and blend until creamy.

2. Lightly coat a large pot with cooking spray. Add the cheese mixture, chicken, and potatoes, and mix gently. Stirring occasionally, heat the mixture over low heat for 10 minutes, or until heated through.

3. Spoon the stew into the bread bowl and serve.

---

* For best results, choose soft ripe cheeses, such as Brie and Camembert; semi-soft varieties, like Fontina, Havarti, Feta, and Blue; and firm cheeses, such as Cheddar, Swiss, Edam, Gouda, and Provolone. The cheese should be at room temperature and free of any waxy coating or rind.

8.Casseroles
inaBowl

Time to say goodbye to your old casserole dish. We've got a new one for you—a fully edible, totally portable, "perfect-for-baking-in" bread bowl! Much easier on the teeth than sorry old glass dishes, bread bowls are the perfect vessels for cooking your favorite casseroles as well as serving them. As an added bonus, the casserole "dish" becomes even more deliciously crisp as it bakes.

Wonderfully warm and comforting, our "casserole-in-a-bread-bowl" recipes are especially good choices when the weather turns brisk and cold. For a taste of hearty down-home goodness, gather your family around the table to enjoy our Chicken Noodle Casserole. Thick with vegetables and noodles, this time-honored classic is both nourishing and delicious. Another satisfying choice is the Tuna Melt Casserole, with its cheesy crown of Cheddar and Monterey Jack. In the mood for a gourmet steak sandwich? Don't pass up the London Broil Coffee-Cup Casserole with its tender strips of beef and sweet bell peppers in a lusciously addictive sauce. The Spaghettini Casserole and Grandma's Goulash are two more rib-sticking choices that are delicious and satisfying, yet easy on the budget. When you're craving something from South of the Border, be sure to try the Mexican Lasagna. Its savory layers of beef and cheese nestled between tortilla chips and flavored with spicy chile sauce will have you singing *Olé.* And the choices go on and on . . .

Whether you're expecting company or serving a quiet dinner at home, the following recipes are sure to please. So replace your baking dish with a crisp, crunchy sourdough bread bowl, and give some of the following casseroles a try.

CHICKEN**NOODLE**CASSEROLE

Nothing says "comfort" better than this heartwarming casserole
that is both delicious and nutritious. A true classic!

YIELD: 4 SERVINGS

3 skinless, boneless
chicken breast halves

I carrot, peeled

2 celery stalks

I medium onion

½ teaspoon dried thyme

½ teaspoon dried rosemary

8 ounces uncooked
wide noodles

Butter for coating
bread bowl

¼ cup butter

3 tablespoons
all-purpose flour

2 teaspoons
Worcestershire sauce

1. Place the chicken, carrot, celery, onion, thyme, and rosemary in a medium pot with enough water to cover. Place over medium-high heat and bring to a boil. Reduce the heat to medium-low and cook for 5 to 7 minutes. Remove the cooked celery and carrot from the pot and let cool.

2. Continue to cook the chicken and onion another 5 to 10 minutes, or until thoroughly cooked, then remove from the pot and let cool. Reserve the broth. When cool enough to handle, cut the chicken and vegetables into bite-sized pieces and set aside.

3. Cook the noodles according to package directions until al dente. Do not overcook. Drain and set aside.

4. Preheat the oven to 350°F. Butter the inside of the bread bowl and set aside.

5. In a medium skillet, melt the ¼ cup butter over medium-low heat. Stirring constantly, add the flour and enough of the broth to form a thick sauce. Continuing to stir, add the Worcestershire sauce, salt, pepper, mushrooms, and half the cheese. Cook about 3 minutes or until thick. Remove from the heat.

6. Place half the noodles on the bottom of the bread bowl. Top with half the chicken and vegetables, and half the sauce. Repeat the layers. Top with the remaining cheese, and sprinkle with paprika.

7. Wrap the bowl with aluminum foil, leaving the top uncovered. Place the bowl on a baking sheet in the middle of the oven, and bake for 12 minutes or until the casserole is heated through. Carefully remove the foil and continue to bake another 3 minutes.

8. To serve, spoon the casserole onto individual plates, then cut the bread bowl into pieces to serve with it.

Salt, to taste

Black pepper, to taste

1/2 cup chopped fresh or canned mushrooms

8 ounces shredded Monterey Jack cheese

1 teaspoon paprika

1- to 1 3/4-pound bread bowl

TUNAMELTCASSEROLE

Can't decide between a tuna casserole and a tuna sandwich?
When a crusty sourdough bread bowl is involved,
the choice is easy!

YIELD: 4 SERVINGS

8 ounces uncooked
elbow macaroni

Butter for coating
bread bowl

¼ cup butter

¼ cup finely chopped onion

2 tablespoons finely
chopped celery

2 tablespoons
all-purpose flour

¾ teaspoon salt

⅛ teaspoon black pepper

I cup milk

I cup condensed cream
of mushroom soup
(without added liquid)

7-ounce can tuna,
drained and flaked

½ cup frozen peas, thawed

½ cup shredded Monterey
Jack cheese

1. In a medium saucepan, cook the macaroni according to package instructions until al dente. Do not overcook. Drain and set aside.

2. Preheat the oven to 350°F. Butter the inside of the bread bowl and set aside.

3. Heat ¼ cup butter in a large saucepan over low heat. Add the onion and celery, and sauté about 3 minutes, or until the onion is soft and translucent.

4. Stirring constantly, add the flour, salt, and pepper to the saucepan. Add the milk and soup, continuing to stir until thickened. Fold in the macaroni, then add the tuna, peas, and half of both cheeses, and mix together well. Remove from the heat.

4. Toss the toasted sourdough bread with the melted butter, and set aside.

5. Spoon the tuna mixture into the bread bowl, top with the remaining cheese and toasted breadcrumbs.

6. Wrap the bowl with aluminum foil, leaving the top uncovered. Place the bowl on a baking sheet in the middle of the oven, and bake for 30 minutes or until the casserole is heated through. Carefully remove the foil and continue to bake another 3 minutes.

7. To serve, spoon the casserole onto individual plates, then cut the bread bowl into pieces to serve with it.

¹/₂ cup shredded Cheddar cheese

1 slice sourdough bread, well toasted and crumbled

2 teaspoons melted butter

1- to 1³/₄-pound bread bowl

LONDONBROIL**COFFEE**-CUP **CASSEROLE**

When Lisa was growing up, her mom's London broil, made with a slightly sweet, slightly tangy, positively addicting sauce, was one of her favorite dishes. Lisa eventually learned the sauce's secret ingredient (and possible cause for its addictive nature)—a double-strength shot of coffee! Just wait until you try it!

1. In a medium bowl, prepare a marinade by combining half the water, 1 teaspoon of coffee, and one bottle of chili sauce in a shallow baking pan. Add the meat and turn to coat well. Cover and marinate in the refrigerator at least four hours, turning the meat occasionally.

YIELD: 4 SERVINGS

1 cup water

2 rounded teaspoons instant coffee

2 bottles (12 ounces each) chili sauce

1 ¹/₂ pound flank steak

2 green bell peppers, cut into chunks

1- to 1³/₄-pound bread bowl

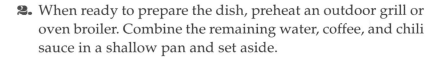

2. When ready to prepare the dish, preheat an outdoor grill or oven broiler. Combine the remaining water, coffee, and chili sauce in a shallow pan and set aside.

3. Cook the meat about 5 to 10 minutes per side, or until cooked to desired doneness, basting often with the marinade. Discard any remaining marinade.

4. Transfer the meat to a cutting board and slice across the grain into thin strips, then halve the strips.

5. Preheat the oven to 350°F.

6. Using a basting brush, baste the inside of the bread bowl with ¼ cup of the sauce. Add the sliced meat, bell pepper, and the remaining sauce. Gently stir the mixture.

7. Wrap the bowl with aluminum foil, leaving the top uncovered. Place the bowl on a baking sheet in the middle of the oven, and bake for 7 minutes or until the casserole is heated through. Carefully remove the foil and continue to bake another 3 minutes.

8. To serve, spoon the casserole onto individual plates, then cut the bread bowl into pieces to serve with it.

CHICKEN**CASSEROLE**WITH **APRICOT**PRESERVES

This easy-to-prepare chicken casserole benefits from the sweetness of apricot preserves and the tangy zip of Thousand Island dressing.

1. Preheat the oven to 350°F.

2. In a medium bowl, combine the preserves, Thousand Island dressing, and soup mix until well blended.

3. Arrange the chicken in a large shallow baking dish, and top with the apricot mixture. Bake uncovered, basting occasionally with pan juices, for 1½ hours or until the chicken is thoroughly cooked and no longer pink inside when cut with a knife. Remove from the oven and allow to cool slightly, then cut into bite-sized pieces.

4. Using a basting brush, baste the inside of the bread bowl with some of the apricot sauce. Spoon the chicken and sauce into the bread bowl.

5. Wrap the bowl with aluminum foil, leaving the top uncovered. Place the bowl on a baking sheet in the middle of the oven, and bake for 12 minutes or until the casserole is heated through. Carefully remove the foil and continue to bake another 3 minutes.

6. To serve, spoon the casserole onto individual plates, then cut the bread bowl into pieces to serve with it.

YIELD: 4 SERVINGS

1 ¼ cup apricot preserves

1 cup Thousand Island dressing

1 envelope (1.38 ounces) dry onion soup mix

6 skinless, boneless chicken breast halves

1- to 1¾-pound bread bowl

SPAGHETTINICASSEROLE

*Dishes like this one were born during the Great Depression,
when meals had to be satisfying yet inexpensive. Don't
be surprised if it becomes one of your family favorites!*

YIELD: 4 SERVINGS

8 ounces uncooked
spaghetti

2 cups homemade or
canned spaghetti sauce

1 tablespoon grated
Parmesan cheese

1 teaspoon vegetable oil

1 medium onion,
chopped

1 1/2 pounds lean
ground beef

1 teaspoon salt

1/2 teaspoon black pepper

1 1/4 teaspoons
Worcestershire sauce

1- to 1 3/4-pound
bread bowl

1. In a medium saucepan, cook the spaghetti according to package instructions until al dente. Do not overcook. Drain and return to the pan. Add the sauce and toss to coat. Sprinkle with cheese and toss again.

2. While the spaghetti cooks, preheat the oven to 350°F. In a large skillet, heat the oil over medium-low heat, add the onion, and sauté for 3 minutes or until translucent.

3. Add the beef, increase the heat to medium, and brown until completely cooked. Remove the skillet from the heat, and drain the excess fat. Add the salt, pepper, and Worcestershire sauce to the beef, and mix well. Add the spaghetti and toss. Spoon the mixture into the bread bowl.

4. Wrap the bowl with aluminum foil, leaving the top uncovered. Place the bowl on a baking sheet in the middle of the oven, and bake for 25 minutes or until the casserole is heated through. Carefully remove the foil and continue to bake another 3 minutes.

5. To serve, spoon the casserole onto individual plates, then cut the bread bowl into pieces to serve with it.

GRANDMA'S**GOULASH**

*This Hungarian-inspired recipe comes from Lisa's grandmother
Helen, an expert cook who prepared many traditional recipes
from her homeland. Occasionally, instead of making the
usual beef or veal goulash, she would prepare this
version made with knockwurst. Pure comfort food!*

1. Preheat the oven to 350°F.

2. Heat the oil in a medium saucepan over medium-low heat.
Add the onion and sauté about 5 minutes, or until soft and
beginning to brown. Turn off the heat and let cool.

3. To the cooled onions, add the potatoes, tomato sauce,
paprika, salt, and enough water to almost cover. Cook the
potatoes slowly over low heat for 30 minutes, stirring occasionally and carefully to avoid breaking the potatoes. Add
the knockwurst and cook about 10 minutes. Spoon the mixture into the bread bowl.

4. Wrap the bowl with aluminum foil, leaving the top uncovered. Place the bowl on a baking sheet in the middle of the
oven, and bake for 12 minutes or until the casserole is
heated through. Carefully remove the foil and continue to
bake another 3 minutes.

5. To serve, spoon the casserole onto individual plates, then
cut the bread bowl into pieces to serve with it.

YIELD: 4 SERVINGS

1 teaspoon vegetable oil

1 medium onion, minced

6 large potatoes, peeled
and cubed

1 cup tomato sauce

2 teaspoons Hungarian
paprika

1 ½ teaspoons salt

4 large knockwurst,
cut into bite-sized slices

1- to 1 ¾-pound bread bowl

SOURDOUGHPAELLA

*This tasty Spanish rice dish typically includes
assorted meats, shellfish, or a combination of both.
It takes its name from the wide, shallow frying
pan traditionally used in its preparation.*

YIELD: **4** SERVINGS

2¹/₂ tablespoons olive oil

1 medium onion, chopped

2 cloves garlic, minced

2 skinless, boneless
chicken breast halves, cut
into thin 1-x-¹/₂-inch strips

³/₄ cup chopped,
peeled tomatoes

¹/₂ teaspoon lemon juice

¹/₄ teaspoon salt

¹/₄ teaspoon black pepper

¹/₂ cup thinly sliced
chorizo sausage

¹/₄ cup bite-sized ham cubes

³/₄ cup chopped green
bell pepper

1 cup uncooked
long grain rice

4 cups chicken broth

8 medium cooked shrimp,
shelled and deveined

1. Preheat the oven to 350°F.

2. Heat the oil in a large skillet, wok, or paella pan over medium-low heat. Add the onion and garlic, and sauté 2 minutes, or until beginning to soften. Add the chicken, tomatoes, lemon juice, salt, and pepper, and simmer for 7 minutes, or until the chicken is thoroughly cooked. Add the chorizo, ham, and bell pepper, and stir well. Continue to cook another 3 minutes.

3. Stir the rice into the skillet, and mix well with the ingredients. Add the broth and shrimp. Crush the saffron, and add to the mixture. Stir well.

4. Bring the ingredients to a boil, then reduce the heat to low. Cover and let simmer for 20 minutes, or until the rice is tender. Gently stir in the sourdough chunks, cover, and simmer another minute. Uncover and stir in the peas and more chicken broth, if needed. Spoon the mixture into the bread bowl.

5. Wrap the bowl with aluminum foil, leaving the top uncovered. Place the bowl on a baking sheet in the middle of the oven, and bake for 7 minutes or until the casserole is heated through. Carefully remove the foil and continue to bake another 3 minutes.

6. To serve, spoon the casserole onto individual plates, then cut the bread bowl into pieces to serve with it.

I thread saffron*

1/4 cup frozen peas, thawed

I cup bread chunks from the hollowed-out bowl

I- to I 3/4-pound bread bowl

---

* If possible, avoid using powdered saffron, which is not as pure and flavorful as the threads.

CHEF**IAN**MORRISON'S**CHILES** RELLENOS**SHRIMP**CASSEROLE

Ian Morrison, award-winning executive chef of Northern California's Corinthian Yacht Club and member of the Tasting Panel of the American Culinary Federation in San Francisco, has created this innovative Mexican-inspired casserole.

YIELD: 4 SERVINGS

2 mild chile peppers
(preferably pasilla)

8 ounces medium shrimp,
shelled and deveined

1 tablespoon butter

2 cloves garlic, chopped

1 ½ teaspoons chile powder

8 ounces Monterey Jack
cheese, shredded

1 tablespoon chopped
fresh cilantro

1 tablespoon chopped
fresh mint

2 cups half-and-half

3 eggs, beaten

¼ teaspoon salt

1 ½ teaspoons lime juice

Diced chile pepper
for garnish

1- to 1¾-pound
bread bowl

1. Preheat the oven to 375°F.

2. To roast the chile peppers,* first heat a large skillet over medium heat. Cut a small slit in each pepper and place them in the hot skillet. Turn the peppers as they blister and char. When completely charred, immediately wrap them in a clean, moist kitchen towel and let cool (this will help loosen their skin). Peel off the skin and slit the chiles with a knife, then remove the seeds and chop. Set aside.

3. Place the shrimp, butter, garlic, and chile powder in the skillet over medium-low heat. Sauté about 3 minutes, or until the shrimp just begins to turn pink. Remove from the heat and set aside.

4. In a medium bowl, toss the Monterey Jack cheese with half of both the cilantro and mint, and set aside. In a separate bowl, combine the half-and-half with the eggs. Add the salt and lime juice, and mix well.

5. Place the shrimp mixture in the bottom of the bread bowl in an even layer, top with the chile peppers, and cover with all but ¼ cup of the cheese mixture. Pour the egg mixture on top, and sprinkle with the remaining cheese.

6. Wrap the bowl with aluminum foil, leaving the top uncovered. Place the bowl on a baking sheet in the middle of the oven, and bake for 25 minutes or until the egg mixture is fully cooked. Carefully remove the foil and continue to bake another 3 minutes.

7. Before serving, garnish with diced chiles and the remaining cilantro and mint. Cut the bread bowl into wedges, and serve.

---

* When preparing the peppers, be sure to wear gloves, and be careful not to touch your eyes.

MEXICANLASAGNA

*Red chile sauce helps pack a punch in this outstanding
Mexican lasagna in which tortilla chips take the
place of traditional noodles. Muy bueno!*

YIELD: 4 SERVINGS

2 pounds ground beef

I medium onion, chopped

I clove garlic, minced

2 cups canned tomatoes

10-ounce can red chile sauce

¾ cup chopped black olives

I teaspoon salt

¼ teaspoon black pepper

½ cup ricotta cheese

I egg

8 ounces Monterey Jack
cheese, thinly sliced

8 ounces tortilla chips

½ cup shredded
Cheddar cheese

1- to 1¾-pound
bread bowl

1. Preheat the oven to 350°F.

2. Brown the beef in a large skillet over medium heat, then
drain the excess fat. Stir in the onion and garlic, and sauté
for 2 minutes or until the onions begin to soften. Add the
tomatoes, chile sauce, olives, salt, and pepper. Increase the
heat and bring to a boil, then reduce the heat to low and
simmer 20 minutes.

3. In a small bowl, combine the ricotta cheese and egg. Set aside.

4. Spoon a third of the meat mixture into the bread bowl. Top
with half the Monterey Jack cheese, half the ricotta mixture,
and a layer of tortilla chips. Repeat the layers, ending with
a third of the meat mixture. Sprinkle the top with Cheddar
cheese.

5. Wrap the bowl with aluminum foil, leaving the top uncovered. Place the bowl on a baking sheet in the middle of the
oven, and bake for 15 minutes or until the casserole is
heated through. Carefully remove the foil and continue to
bake another 3 minutes.

6. To serve, spoon the casserole onto individual plates, then
cut the bread bowl into pieces to serve with it.

9.Main**Course** Creations

Hearty stews and delectable casseroles are not the only types of entrées that are "bread-bowl worthy." Some of your favorite main courses can make delightful presentations when served in crunchy bread bowls. Just about any type of food works, whether grilled, poached, stir-fried, broiled, or baked. The recipes in this chapter are easy-to-prepare and range from gourmet presentations to casual affairs. To satisfy a wide variety of tastes, we offer selections that spotlight chicken, turkey, fish, lamb, and beef. Something for everyone!

When time is at a premium, the Barbecued Chicken Pizza Bowl or Shrimp with Saffron Cream Sauce will allow you to get dinner on the table in a matter of minutes. Another time-saving choice is the Turkey Breast Putanesca, a dish in which moist slices of turkey are tossed in a Mediterranean-flavored tomato sauce. When only comfort food will fill the bill, try the Southwestern Shepherd's Pie with its delectable chipotle mashed potato topping. Expecting guests for dinner? You'll be proud to serve the Dijon Mustard Chicken Breast. This creation of award-winning Chef John Kane pairs broccoli florets and breaded chicken breasts under a blanket of heavenly Dijon sauce. And for a taste of New Orleans, the Baked Muffuletta Dinner Sandwich—baked right in the bread bowl—is a sure winner.

Bread bowls have certainly come a long way from simply housing soups and dips. The main-dish recipes on the following pages are proof. And remember—don't limit yourself to the selections in this book. Try serving your own favorite entrées in these delectable bread bowl containers.

LEMON-GARLIC
BARBECUED**LAMB**

A bread bowl serves as the perfect house for this delectably
seasoned grilled lamb and vegetable medley.

YIELD: 4 SERVINGS

1 ½ pounds lean lamb or beef,
cut into bite-sized pieces

1 ½ tablespoons olive oil

2 cups spinach

1 teaspoon dried thyme

1 teaspoon dried rosemary

12 cherry tomatoes

12 pearl onions

1 ½ cups barbecue sauce

1- to 1 ¾-pound bread bowl

MARINADE
½ cup olive oil

½ cup red wine

Juice of 1 lemon

3 cloves garlic, minced

1 tablespoon dried oregano

Salt, to taste

Black pepper, to taste

1. Combine all of the marinade ingredients in shallow pan. Add the meat, turning to coat well. Cover and refrigerate at least 5 hours, turning the meat occasionally.

2. When ready to prepare the dish, preheat an outdoor grill or oven broiler.

3. Heat the oil in a medium skillet over medium-low heat. Add the spinach, thyme, and rosemary, and sauté for 3 minutes, or until the spinach begins wilt. Remove from the heat and set aside.

4. Alternate the meat, tomatoes, and onions on skewers. Cook, turning frequently, for 10 minutes or until the meat is cooked to the desired doneness. Carefully remove the food from the skewers. Discard any remaining marinade.

5. Using a basting brush, lightly baste the inside of the bread bowl with barbecue sauce. Place the spinach in the bottom of the bowl, then add the lamb, tomatoes, and onions. Serve immediately with barbecue sauce on the side.

SOUTHWESTERN
SHEPHERD'S**PIE**

*Heavenly mashed potatoes are always a welcomed treat; but in
this dish, chipotle peppers elevate them to flavorful new heights.*

1. Heat the oil in a large skillet over medium heat. Add the
beef, and cook about 10 minutes or until well browned.
Sprinkle with ½ teaspoon of the chile powder, and continue
to cook a minute.

2. Add the tomato puree, onion, carrots, chile pepper, and garlic to the skillet. Cook for a minute, then add the remaining
chile powder, the cumin, beef stock, and lime juice. Bring
the ingredients to a boil, then reduce the heat to low. Cover
and simmer 1 hour or until the beef is tender.

3. Preheat the broiler.

4. To prepare the mashed potatoes, place the potatoes in a
medium saucepan with enough water to cover, and bring to
a boil. Cook about 20 minutes or until tender. Transfer to a
medium bowl, and mash with the half-and-half, salt, and
pepper, and half the butter. Stir in the minced chipotle.

5. Spoon the beef mixture into the bread bowl, and top with
the mashed potatoes. Brush the top with the remaining butter, and place under the broiler for 3 minutes or until the
top is browned. Serve immediately.

YIELD: 4 SERVINGS

1 tablespoon olive oil

1 pound beef stew meat

1 teaspoon chile powder

8-ounce can tomato puree

1 medium onion, chopped

2 carrots, coarsely chopped

1 pasilla chile pepper, or
other mild chile, julienned*

2 garlic cloves, chopped

1 tablespoon ground cumin

1 cup beef stock

1 tablespoon lime juice

1- to 1¾-pound bread bowl

POTATO TOPPING

3 medium potatoes,
peeled and cut into chunks

1¼ cups half-and-half

Salt, to taste

Black pepper, taste

3 tablespoons butter

1 chipotle chile pepper, or other
medium-hot chile, minced*

*When preparing the peppers, be
sure to wear gloves, and be careful
not to touch your eyes.

CALIFORNIA-STYLE BARBECUED**CHICKEN** **PIZZA**BOWL

Pizza topped with juicy barbecued chicken, bits of red onion,
and fresh cilantro is practically a California staple.
Your sourdough bread bowl replaces the pizza
crust in this luscious dinnertime meal.

<u>YIELD:</u> **4** SERVINGS

4 skinless, boneless
chicken breasts,
cooked and shredded

1 ½ cups barbecue sauce

1 ½ tablespoons honey

¼ cup brown sugar

¾ cup chopped fresh cilantro

1 ¼ cups thinly sliced
green bell pepper

1 cup shredded
mozzarella cheese

2 tablespoons shredded
smoked Gouda cheese
(optional)

¾ cup thinly sliced red onion

1- to 1 ¾-pound bread bowl

1. Preheat the broiler.

2. Combine the chicken, barbecue sauce, honey, brown sugar, cilantro, and green pepper in a medium saucepan and bring to a boil over medium heat.

3. Spoon the mixture into the bread bowl, and top with the cheeses and onion.

4. Place under the broiler for 3 minutes, or until the cheese melts and begins to brown. Serve immediately.

CHICKEN'N'SOURDOUGH
DUMPLINGS

*When it's comfort food you're craving, look no further than
this heartwarming dish. A blend of cinnamon, rosemary,
and dill offer a uniquely flavorful twist to the "dumplings."*

1. Place the chicken, water, broth, carrots, onion, celery, garlic, salt, and pepper in a large stockpot and bring to a boil. Reduce the heat to low, cover, and simmer 1 hour.

2. Remove the chicken from the pot and place on a large plate to cool. When cool enough to handle, remove the meat from the bones and return it to the pot of simmering broth along with the sausage.

3. To prepare the "dumplings," squeeze chunks of the sourdough bread with your hands to form about 8 dumplings. Set aside.

4. In a small bowl, mix together the cinnamon, rosemary, and dill. Roll the dumplings in the spice mixture, gently pressing the spices into the bread.

5. Spoon the chicken mixture into the bread bowl, and add the dumplings just before serving.

YIELD: 4 SERVINGS

1 whole chicken
(about 2½ pounds)

5 cups water

3 cups chicken broth

2 carrots, coarsely chopped

1 medium yellow onion,
coarsely chopped

2 stalks celery, coarsely
chopped

1 clove garlic, finely chopped

1 teaspoon salt

1 teaspoon black pepper

¾ cup cooked Italian sweet
sausage, crumbled

1- to 1¾-pound bread bowl

DUMPLINGS

Half the bread from the
hollowed-out bowl

1¼ teaspoons ground
cinnamon

1¼ teaspoons dried rosemary

1¼ teaspoons dried dill

TURKEYBREASTPUTANESCA

*Putanesca—the famous pasta sauce flavored with
anchovies and capers—tops moist slices of turkey breast
in this hearty dish. The incomparable taste of the
sauce-soaked bread bowl defies description.*

YIELD: 4 SERVINGS

4 tablespoons olive oil

1 ½ pounds thinly sliced
turkey breast

¼ cup finely chopped
yellow onion

3 cloves garlic, peeled
and crushed

4 whole anchovies,
or 1 tablespoon paste

3 cups tomato sauce

1 tablespoon capers

¼ cup chopped
kalamata olives

1 pinch red pepper flakes

Chopped Italian parsley
for garnish

Freshly grated Parmesan or
Romano cheese for garnish

1- to 1 ¾-pound bread bowl

1. Heat 2 tablespoons of the oil in a large skillet over medium heat. Add the turkey and cook until the slices are cooked through and no longer pink. Transfer to a platter and set aside.

2. Heat the remaining oil in the skillet, add the onion, and sauté 5 minutes or until soft and translucent. Add the garlic and sauté another minute. Toss in the anchovies and mash with a fork.

3. Stir the tomato sauce into the skillet, and simmer the ingredients for 5 minutes. If the sauce is too thick, add a little wine or stock to reach the desired consistency. Add the capers, olives, and pepper flakes, stirring to mix thoroughly. Simmer another 5 minutes.

4. Cut the turkey into bite-sized pieces, add to the sauce, and mix well. Spoon the mixture into the bread bowl, garnish with parsley and cheese, and serve.

SHRIMPWITHSAFFRON CREAMSAUCE

Saffron is one of the world's most treasured spices,
adding pungent, aromatic flavor and
a warm golden hue to dishes.

YIELD: 4 SERVINGS

1 teaspoon saffron threads

2 tablespoons olive oil

1 shallot, minced fine

2 cloves garlic, minced fine

$\frac{1}{2}$ cup white wine

1 pint heavy cream

2 pounds cooked medium shrimp

Chopped parsley for garnish

1- to 1$\frac{3}{4}$-pound bread bowl

1. Toast the saffron lightly in a medium skillet over low heat for 1 to 2 minutes, being careful not to burn it. With the back of a spoon, crush the saffron into a powder. Add the oil, shallot, and garlic, and cook over low heat for 2 minutes, or until the shallots are soft and translucent. Turn off the heat.

2. Gently stir the wine and cream into the skillet. Continuing to stir, return the heat to medium and bring the ingredients to a boil. Continue to stir about 3 minutes, or until the sauce is thick and coats the back of a spoon.

3. Add the shrimp, reduce the heat to low, and simmer for another 2 minutes.

4. Spoon the mixture into the bread bowl, garnish with parsley, and serve.

POACHED**SALMON**WITH **MUSTARD**-DILL**SAUCE**

*Although we typically prepare this dish with fresh King salmon
caught by our friends off the Northern California coast,
any fresh salmon will do.*

YIELD: 4 SERVINGS

3 cups water

¼ teaspoon salt

4 black peppercorns

3 lemon slices

3 parsley sprigs

I small onion, sliced

I bay leaf

2 pounds salmon fillets

I- to I ¾-pound bread bowl

MUSTARD-DILL SAUCE

¾ cup sour cream

¼ cup Dijon mustard

I teaspoon chopped fresh dill

I teaspoon lemon juice

I teaspoon honey

1. Bring the water to boil in a large deep skillet. Stirring slowly, add the salt, peppercorns, lemon slices, parsley, onion, and bay leaf. Reduce the heat to low, cover, and simmer about 5 minutes.

2. Carefully add the salmon to the skillet, adding more water if necessary to just cover. Simmer uncovered for 12 to 15 minutes, or until the salmon is cooked and flakes easily with a fork. Remove to a platter, and flake into large pieces.

3. While the salmon cooks, blend the sauce ingredients in a small mixing bowl. Set aside.

4. Remove and discard the bay leaf. Place one-fourth of the salmon in the bottom of the bread bowl, and top with one-fourth of the sauce. Repeat the layers, ending with the sauce.

5. Cut the bread bowl into four wedges and serve.

BAKED**MUFFULETTA** **DINNER**SANDWICH

*Second only to New Orlean's famous Po'Boy, the muffuletta is
a rustic sandwich of assorted cold cuts and cheese topped with
mouthwatering olive salad. Our giant-sized version, which serves
four, is prepared on a sourdough round, baked, and served hot.*

1. Preheat the oven to 350°F.

2. To prepare the olive spread, place the green and black
olives, garlic, celery, parsley, and scallions in a food processor, and pulse until well minced, but not pureed. Transfer to
a bowl, and stir in the olive oil, vinegar, black pepper, and
Tabasco sauce. Mix well.

3. Cut the sourdough round in half, so it resembles a large
hamburger bun. Remove enough bread from the top and
bottom halves to create a pocket for holding the cold cuts
and cheese. Spread both halves with the olive spread, then
fill the bottom half with slices of mortadella, salami, ham,
and provolone. Cover with the top half of the round.

4. Wrap the entire bowl with aluminum foil. Place on a baking
sheet in the middle of the oven and bake for 12 minutes, or
until the sandwich is heated through. Carefully remove the
foil and continue to bake another 3 minutes.

5. Once it is cool enough to handle, cut the muffuletta into
quarters and serve.

YIELD: 4 SERVINGS

¼ pound sliced mortadella (Italian-style bologna)

¼ pound sliced salami

¼ pound sliced ham

¼ pound sliced provolone cheese

1- to 1¾ pound sourdough round (not hollowed out)

OLIVE SPREAD

1 cup pimento-stuffed green olives

½ cup black pitted olives

1 clove garlic

¼ cup chopped celery

¼ cup chopped Italian flat-leaf parsley

¼ cup chopped scallions

½ cup olive oil

1 teaspoon red wine vinegar

½ teaspoon freshly ground black pepper

6 dashes Tabasco sauce, or to taste

CHEFJOHNKANE'S DIJONMUSTARDCHICKEN BREAST

*John Kane, award-winning executive chef of San Francisco's
prestigious University Club, has created this exceptional entrée in
which an incomparable Dijon sauce blankets broccoli florets and
juicy pieces of crumb-coated chicken. Outstanding!*

YIELD: **4** SERVINGS

4 tablespoons butter

2 garlic cloves, minced

¼ cup Dijon mustard

2 cups sourdough
breadcrumbs*

¼ cup minced parsley

½ cup grated Parmesan
cheese

4 skinless, boneless
chicken breast halves

1 ¼ cups cooked
broccoli florets

Minced parsley for garnish

1- to 1 ¾-pound
bread bowl

*To make breadcrumbs from the
hollowed-out bowl, see page 13.

1. Melt the butter in a medium skillet over low heat. Add the
garlic and sauté 5 minutes, or until soft. Stir in the mustard
and blend well. Remove from the heat and let cool to the
touch, but do not let solidify. Using a whisk or fork, whip the
mixture vigorously until it thickens and does not separate.

2. Place the breadcrumbs, parsley, and half the Parmesan in a
medium bowl and mix well.

3. Dip each chicken breast in the butter mixture, then roll in
the breadcrumb mixture. Press the crumbs onto the breasts
to coat well. Place the chicken in a large pan, cover, and
refrigerate at least 2 hours.

4. Preheat the oven to 350°F. Spray a baking sheet with nonstick cooking spray.

5. Arrange the chicken on the baking sheet and bake for 45
minutes to 1 hour, or until thoroughly cooked. Leaving the

oven on, transfer the chicken to a cutting board and slice into bite-sized pieces.

6. Blend the sauce ingredients together in a small bowl, and spread a small amount on the inside of the bread bowl.

7. Place the broccoli in the bottom of the bread bowl, top with the chicken, and sprinkle with the remaining Parmesan cheese. Top with the sauce and garnish with parsley.

8. Wrap the bowl with aluminum foil, leaving the top uncovered. Place the bowl on a baking sheet in the middle of the oven, and bake about 12 minutes or until heated through. Carefully remove the foil and continue to bake another 3 minutes. Serve immediately.

DIJON SAUCE

¼ cup Dijon mustard

¼ cup mayonnaise

1 teaspoon honey

10.Show-**Stopping** Sides

Although entrées may be the stars of a meal, side dishes can be taste-tempting creations that are just as worthy of standing ovations. And when they are served in edible bread bowls that deliciously absorb the flavors within, everyone will take notice.

In this chapter, we serve up some outstanding recipes for super sides that become even more exceptional when presented in sourdough bowls. Fresh vegetables, as well as hearty beans and grains are all represented. Sautéed scallions in a velvety bacon-studded garlic sauce are spotlighted in our Creamed Green Onions with Parmesan and Bacon, while fresh tomatoes, zucchini, garlic, and basil are tossed with spices, then baked up in a warm Bread Bowl Bruschetta. Delicious! Who hasn't enjoyed fresh bread that has been slathered with a favorite sauce or spread? Our Pesto Mushroom Sauté comes in a bowl that is lined with pungent garlicky pesto, while maple syrup kisses the crisp sourdough that surrounds the delectable Creamed Corn Fritter Casserole. If you love garlic bread (and who doesn't?), you're going to flip over the Cheesy Garlic Bread. And if cheese is your "thing," try the Three-Cheese Spinach Bake with its heavenly blend of Roquefort, feta, and mozzarella melted over a bed of fresh sautéed spinach; or the Pancetta, Coucous 'n' Cheese—a masterful side dish from the recipe files of award-winning Chef Bruce Paton.

Delicious, easy to prepare, and fun to serve, the show-stopping side dishes on the following pages are gastronomic delights. You'll find yourself serving them time and time again.

CHEESYGARLIC**BREAD**

*If you like garlic bread, you'll flip over this cross-cut sourdough
round that is stuffed with a delectable wine-infused cheese
and garlic filling, and then baked to a fabulous crunch.*

YIELD: **10** SERVINGS

1- to 1³/₄-pound sourdough round (not hollowed out)

1 ¹/₄ cups shredded Cheddar cheese

1 ¹/₄ cups shredded mozzarella cheese

2 cloves garlic, minced

2 tablespoons red wine

Chopped chives for garnish

1. Preheat the oven to 350°F.

2. Cut slices into the bread round about 1 inch apart, without cutting through to the bottom. Make a half turn with the round and, once again, cut slices into the bread. This will create 1-x-1-inch square pieces of bread projecting from the center of the loaf (but still attached to the bottom).

3. In a medium bowl, combine the Cheddar and mozzarella cheeses, garlic, and wine. Stuff this mixture between the cut pieces of bread.

4. Wrap the entire loaf in aluminum foil, then place it on a baking sheet in the middle of the oven. Bake for 25 minutes, or until the bread is thoroughly heated and the cheese is melted. Carefully remove the foil and continue to bake another 3 minutes. Remove from the oven and sprinkle with chives.

5. Once cool enough to handle, pull pieces of bread from the bowl and enjoy.

BREAD**BOWL**BRUSCHETTA

*Here's our take on Italian bruschetta—
a flavorful mix of fresh tomatoes, onion, basil,
and garlic traditionally served on toasted bread.*

YIELD: **8** SERVINGS

1. Preheat the oven to 350°F.

2. Place the tomatoes, zucchini, onion, basil, garlic, salt, pepper, and olive oil in a large bowl, and mix well. Set aside.

3. Using the back of a tablespoon, spread the ricotta on the inside of the bread bowl, then add the tomato mixture. Wrap the bowl with aluminum foil, leaving the top uncovered. Place the bowl on a baking sheet in the middle of the oven, and bake for 25 minutes or until the filling is heated.

4. Carefully remove the foil. Sprinkle the top with mozzarella cheese, and place under the broiler for 2 to 3 minutes, or until the cheese melts and is golden brown.

5. Spoon the bruschetta onto individual plates, and serve with pieces of the bread bowl.

6 large fresh tomatoes, cut into bite-sized pieces

4 small zucchini, peeled and diced (about 3 cups)

3/4 cup chopped red onion

1/4 cup chopped fresh basil

2 cloves garlic, minced

Salt, to taste

Black pepper, to taste

3/4 cup olive oil

1/2 cup ricotta cheese

3/4 cup shredded mozzarella cheese

1- to 1 3/4-pound bread bowl

CREAMED**CORN** **FRITTER**CASSEROLE

Corn fritters and creamed corn unite in this
memorable side dish that is pure heaven.

YIELD: 6 SERVINGS

5 cups cooked corn
kernels

I cup milk

I cup heavy cream

2 ½ tablespoons sugar

I teaspoon salt

³⁄₄ teaspoon black pepper

½ teaspoon dried thyme

I clove garlic, minced

I stick unsalted butter

2 tablespoons
all-purpose flour

½ cup pure maple syrup

I- to I-³⁄₄-pound
bread bowl

1. To prepare the fritters, sift together the baking mix and baking powder in a medium bowl and set aside. In another bowl, mix together the creamed corn and egg, then add to the baking mixture. Stir gently to combine.

2. Heat the oil in a large deep skillet over medium heat. Carefully drop rounded tablespoons of batter into the hot oil and fry about 2 minutes on each side or until golden brown. Transfer to paper towels. When cool enough to handle, crumble into bite-sized chunks.

3. Preheat the oven to 350°F.

4. Combine the corn kernels, milk, cream, sugar, salt, pepper, thyme, and garlic in a large saucepan over medium heat and bring to a boil. Reduce the heat to low and simmer for 5 minutes.

5. Melt the butter in a medium saucepan over low heat. Stirring constantly, add the flour until well blended, then add to the simmering corn mixture. Continuing to stir, simmer the mixture another 5 minutes or until it thickens. Remove from the heat.

6. Using a tablespoon or basting brush, spread the maple syrup on the inside of the bread bowl. Spoon one-fourth of the creamed corn in the bottom of the bowl, and top with one-fourth of the crumbled fritters. Repeat the layers, ending with the fritters.

7. Wrap the entire bowl with aluminum foil, place on a baking sheet in the middle of the oven, and bake about 20 minutes or until the filling is heated through. Carefully remove the foil and continue to bake another 3 minutes. Serve hot.

CORN FRITTERS

1 ⅓ cups buttermilk baking mix

1 ½ teaspoons baking powder

1 can (14.75 ounce) cream-style corn

1 egg, beaten

1 ¼ cups vegetable oil

THREE-CHEESE**SPINACH**BAKE

*Sautéed spinach is blanketed under a trio of cheese as
its edible serving bowl bakes to crisp perfection.*

YIELD: 6 SERVINGS

1 ½ cups finely chopped
onions

¾ cup crumbled
feta cheese

¼ cup crumbled
Roquefort cheese

2 tablespoons chopped
fresh dill

¼ cup breadcrumbs*

¼ cup olive oil

8 cups coarsely chopped
spinach

¾ cup shredded
mozzarella cheese

1- to 1¾-pound
bread bowl

---

*To make breadcrumbs from the
hollowed-out bowl, see page 13.

1. Preheat the oven to 350°F.

2. Place the onions, feta, Roquefort, dill, and breadcrumbs in a
large bowl and mix well. Set aside.

3. Heat the oil in a large deep skillet over medium heat. Add
the spinach and sauté about 3 minutes, or until just wilted.
Transfer the spinach to a strainer and drain well.

4. Layer half the spinach in the bottom of the bread bowl, and
top with half the cheese-breadcrumb mixture. Repeat the
layers.

5. Wrap the bowl with aluminum foil, leaving the top uncovered. Place the bowl on a baking sheet in the middle of the
oven, and bake for 12 minutes or until the filling is heated
through. Sprinkle with mozzarella. Carefully remove the
foil and continue to bake another 3 minutes.

6. Spoon the spinach mixture onto individual plates along
with pieces of the bread bowl, or cut the filled bowl into
wedges and serve.

CREAMEDGREENONIONS
WITHPARMESANANDBACON

*Sautéed green onions (scallions) are folded into a creamy
bacon-studded garlic sauce and topped with
a sprinkling of Parmesan cheese.*

1. Preheat the broiler.

2. Place the cream, bacon, and garlic in a medium skillet over medium heat, and bring to a boil. Reduce the heat to low and simmer the ingredients, stirring briskly and frequently about 7 minutes, or until the liquid is reduced by half. Remove from the heat.

3. While the mixture is simmering, place the onions and water in a medium saucepan over medium-high heat. Cover and cook about 8 minutes or until the onions are tender.

4. Stir the cream mixture into the onions and add the parsley. Continue to stir the mixture for a minute, or until hot and well blended.

5. Spoon the mixture into the bread bowl and sprinkle with Parmesan cheese. Place under the broiler for a minute or two, or until the cheese is light golden brown.

6. Spoon the green onions onto individual plates and serve with pieces of the bread bowl.

YIELD: 6 SERVINGS

1 cup heavy cream

2 strips crisp bacon, chopped

$1/4$ teaspoon minced garlic

50 green onions (approximately), trimmed and cut in $1/2$-inch pieces

$1/4$ cup water

1 tablespoon chopped fresh parsley

3 tablespoons grated Parmesan cheese

1- to $1\,3/4$-pound bread bowl

EGGPLANT AND TOMATO
CUSTARD

This phenomenal Greek-inspired dish comes from the recipe files of John's mom, a retired professional chef.

YIELD: 6 SERVINGS

YIELD: 6 SERVINGS

1 pound eggplant

Salt for sprinkling on eggplant slices

Olive oil for basting the eggplant

1/4 cup freshly grated Parmesan cheese

1- to 1 3/4-pound bread bowl

TOMATO CUSTARD

2 tablespoons olive oil

1 small onion, minced

1 cup canned tomatoes, drained and chopped

3/4 teaspoon tomato paste

1/4 teaspoon salt

1/4 teaspoon ground cinnamon

1/8 teaspoon ground allspice

1/8 teaspoon ground oregano

1. Preheat the broiler. Lightly oil a baking sheet and set aside.

2. To prepare the tomato custard, heat the oil in a medium skillet over low heat. Add the onion and sauté about 3 minutes, or until soft and translucent. Add the tomatoes, tomato paste, salt, cinnamon, allspice, and oregano, and simmer for 25 minutes while stirring occasionally.

3. While the sauce simmers, slice the eggplant into 1/2-inch thick rounds. Sprinkle with salt, and layer in a colander that is set over a bowl. Let stand 30 minutes, then rinse the slices and pat dry with paper towels.

4. Arrange the eggplant slices on the baking sheet in a single layer. Brush lightly with olive oil and broil about 3 minutes on each side until golden brown. Transfer to paper towels. (This may have to be done in more than one batch.)

5. Preheat the oven to 325°F.

6. To finish preparing the custard, melt the butter in a small saucepan over low heat. Add the flour and whisk constantly until golden brown, but not dark. Remove from

the heat and add the milk in a slow steady stream, whisking constantly until smooth. Add the tomato sauce mixture, continuing to stir for 15 minutes, or until thickened. Remove from the heat, stir in the nutmeg and pepper. Let cool.

7. In a large bowl, combine the egg and ricotta cheese, and whisk into the cooled sauce until well blended.

8. Place half the tomato custard into the bottom of the bread bowl. Top with half the eggplant slices, and sprinkle with half the Parmesan cheese. Cover with the remaining custard, add the remaining eggplant, then spoon the ricotta mixture on top. Sprinkle with rest of the Parmesan.

9. Wrap the bowl with aluminum foil, leaving the top uncovered. Place the bowl on a baking sheet in the middle of the oven, and bake for 12 minutes or until the filling is heated through. Carefully remove the foil and continue to bake another 3 minutes.

10. Let stand 10 minutes before cutting into wedges and serving.

I tablespoon unsalted butter

I tablespoon all-purpose flour

$1/2$ cup milk

Grated nutmeg, to taste

Black pepper, to taste

I large egg, beaten lightly

$1/2$ cup ricotta cheese

FRESH**PEAS**WITH**THYME**

*The thyme-flavored blend of pearl onions and fresh peas makes
a great side dish and wonderful bread bowl filling.*

2 tablespoons butter

2 cloves garlic, chopped

2 ½ cups fresh peas, or
frozen and thawed*

2 cups pearl onions

⅔ cup chicken broth

1 ½ teaspoons chopped
fresh thyme

½ teaspoon salt, or to taste

Black pepper, to taste

1- to 1 ¾-pound bread bowl

---

*If using frozen peas, drain them well
once thawed, and reduce the amount
of broth by 2 tablespoons.

1. Melt the butter in a large saucepan over medium heat. Add
the garlic and sauté about 2 minutes or until golden.

2. Add the peas, onions, broth, and thyme, and bring to a boil.
Reduce the heat to low, and simmer uncovered about 8 minutes or until the onions are tender. Add the salt.

3. Spoon the mixture into the into the bread bowl, sprinkle
with pepper, and serve.

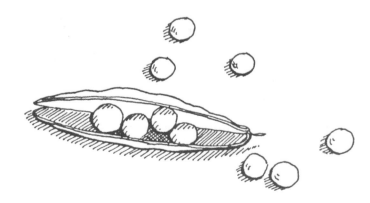

PESTOMUSHROOM**SAUTÉ**

Garlicky basil pesto lends incredible flavor to this mushroom
medley—a magnificent addition to any dinner table.

1. Preheat the oven to 350°F.

2. Heat the oil in a large, deep skillet over medium-low heat. Add the onion and garlic, and cook 3 minutes, or until the onion begins to soften. Add the celery, zucchini, mushrooms, and pepper. Cook 7 minutes, or until the mushrooms are tender and the liquid has nearly evaporated.

3. Using the back of a tablespoon, spread a thin layer of pesto on the inside of the bread bowl. Place in the oven for 3 minutes until heated.

4. Spoon the mushroom mixture into the bread bowl and serve.

YIELD: 6 SERVINGS

1 ½ tablespoons olive oil

¼ cup chopped onion

1 clove garlic, minced

2 stalks celery, chopped

½ cup chopped zucchini

1 pound mixed fresh mushrooms,* sliced

½ teaspoon black pepper

2 ½ tablespoons pesto

1- to 1 ¾-pound bread bowl

---

* Suggested mushroom varieties include crimini, button, shiitake, porcini, and portabella.

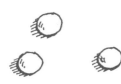

BOSTONBAKED**BEAN**BOWL

*A bread bowl is the perfect serving vessel for this winning
side dish in which navy beans are slow-cooked
in a flavorful sweet, tangy sauce.*

YIELD: 6 SERVINGS

2 cups dry navy beans

8 cups cold water
for soaking beans

6 cups water
for cooking beans

$1/2$ teaspoon salt

8 ounces sliced bacon
or 4 ounces salt pork,
fully cooked, but not crisp

1 medium onion,
chopped

1- to 1$3/4$-pound
bread bowl

1. Rinse the beans and place them in a large pot or bowl with 8 cups cold water. Allow the beans to soak at least 4 hours or overnight.

2. Drain the soaked beans, rinse, and place in a pot along with 6 cups fresh water. Add the salt and bring to a boil. Reduce the heat to medium-low, cover, and simmer gently for 1$1/2$ hours, or until the beans are partially tender. Drain the beans, reserving the cooking liquid.

3. Preheat the oven to 325°F.

4. Layer half the beans in a large casserole dish, top with half the bacon, and sprinkle with half the onion. Repeat the layers, and set aside.

5. Place all of the sauce ingredients in a small pan over medium-high heat. Stirring gently, bring to a boil, then pour over the beans in the casserole dish. Add enough of the reserved liquid to cover the beans.

6. Cover the casserole dish and bake for 1 to 1½ hours, or until the beans are nearly tender. Remove from the oven. If the beans are too dry, stir in a little more liquid.

7. Spoon the beans into the bread bowl. Wrap the bowl with aluminum foil, leaving the top uncovered. Place the bowl on a baking sheet in the middle of the oven, and bake for 25 minutes or until the beans are tender. Carefully remove the foil and continue to bake another 3 minutes. Serve hot.

SAUCE

¼ cup molasses

¼ cup brown sugar

2½ tablespoons ketchup

½ tablespoon Worcestershire sauce

½ teaspoon dry mustard

½ teaspoon salt

CHEFBRUCEPATON'SPANCETTA, COUSCOUS'N'CHEESE

Award-winning executive chef Bruce Paton—chairman of the board of directors for the Chefs Association of the Pacific Coast and the San Francisco chapter of the American Culinary Federation—shares his gourmet take on macaroni and cheese.

YIELD: 6 SERVINGS

2 cups chicken broth

2 ounces pancetta, diced

1 tablespoon olive oil

1/2 cup minced onion

1/2 cup minced celery

1 tablespoon minced garlic

1 cup couscous

8 ounces mascarpone cheese

8 ounces Cheddar cheese, grated

Salt, to taste

Black pepper, to taste

2 tablespoons breadcrumbs*

1- to 1 3/4-pound bread bowl

*To make breadcrumbs from the hollowed-out bowl, see page 13.

1. Bring the chicken broth to a simmer in a medium saucepan over low heat.

2. Cook the pancetta in a heavy-bottomed medium saucepan over low heat for 5 minutes or until crisp. Using a slotted spoon, transfer the pancetta to paper towels.

3. Add the olive oil, onion, celery, and garlic to the saucepan. Sauté about 5 minutes, or until the onion is soft and translucent. Stir in the couscous, then add the hot broth. Cover and simmer about 7 minutes, or until the couscous is cooked and has absorbed the liquid.

4. Gently mix the mascarpone cheese, Cheddar cheese, and pancetta with the couscous, and heat the mixture about 3 minutes, or until the cheese is melted. Season with salt and pepper.

5. Spoon the mixture into the bread bowl and top with the breadcrumbs. Place under the broiler for a minute to brown the crumbs. Serve hot.

11.Desserts to End It All

Bread bowls and desserts? An unlikely duo? Get ready to be pleasantly surprised. Although using hollowed-out sourdough rounds to house desserts may seem a bit unusual, think about it. You spread sweet fruit jams and jellies on your toast, don't you? In the same way, many recipes that include juicy fruits, sweet sauces, and other dessert-type items make wonderful bread bowl fillers.

Take fondues, for example. What began as pots of bubbling cheese into which chunks of French bread were dipped, fondues grew to include a variety of interesting mixtures. Once dessert fondues were introduced, fresh fruits, toasted bread cubes, and ladyfingers were skewered onto forks and immersed into bubbling pots of delectable chocolate or caramel-based blends. Piping hot and gooey good, our S'mores Sourdough Fondue features chocolate sauce, marshmallow creme, and crumbled graham crackers.

Other dessert choices include the Mimosa Bowl, a dessert "cocktail" brimming with fruit that has been steeped in champagne and then layered between heavenly clouds of whipped cream. The innovative Caramel Apple Casserole is our tribute to caramel apples on a stick, while liqueur-soaked cubes of sourdough bread deliver a loaded punch to the After-Dinner Vanilla Parfait. And if you love rich, creamy desserts, Chef Chris Vrattos's Sourdough Bread Pudding is a must-try.

So the next time a special dessert is in order, whether to cap off a gourmet dinner or to celebrate a notable event with family or friends, consider one of the following recipes. They are all special.

S'MORES SOURDOUGH
FONDUE

*Instead of sitting around a campfire, you'll be gathered
around a crunchy fondue "pot," dipping chunks of
fresh fruit and pieces of sourdough bread into this
chocolaty sea with its swirls of marshamallow and
crunchy bits of graham crackers. S'more, please.*

YIELD: 8 SERVINGS

4-ounce package sweet
baking chocolate,
broken into pieces

4 ounces semi-sweet
chocolate chips

$2/3$ cup light cream or milk

$1/2$ cup confectioners'
(powdered) sugar

$1/2$ cup marshmallow creme

I cup medium-sized
graham cracker crumbs

Fresh fruit chunks
for dipping

Bread from the
hollowed-out bowl,
cut into bite-sized cubes

1- to 1 $3/4$-pound bread bowl

1. Place the baking chocolate, chocolate chips, cream, and sugar in a large saucepan or double boiler over low heat. Stir gently but frequently about 3 minutes, or until the chocolate is melted and the mixture is smooth. Remove from the heat.

2. Stir the marshmallow creme and graham cracker crumbs into the chocolate, then pour into the bread bowl.

3. Serve immediately with fruit and bread for dipping.

MIMOSABOWL

A champagne-soaked blend of fresh citrus fruit is wrapped in
a heavenly cloud of whipped cream in this refreshing dessert.

YIELD: 4 SERVINGS

I cup fresh orange sections

I cup fresh tangerine
sections

I cup fresh grapefruit
sections

1/2 cup champagne

1 1/2 cups whipped cream

Ground cinnamon for garnish

1- to 1 3/4-pound bread bowl

1. Place the orange, tangerine, and grapefruit sections in a medium bowl, and gently mix. Pour the champagne on top, cover, and refrigerate 1 to 3 hours.

2. Layer one-third of the whipped cream in the bottom of the bread bowl, and top with half the fruit mixture. Repeat the layers, finishing with a layer of whipped cream.

3. Sprinkle with cinnamon before serving.

CARAMELAPPLE**CASSEROLE**

This innovative dessert is a tribute to those gooey caramel
apples on sticks—once a standard autumn-time treat.

YIELD: 4 SERVINGS

14-ounce package
caramels

1/4 cup heavy cream

3 cups Granny apple slices,
unpeeled

3/4 cup chopped pecans

3/4 cup chocolate-covered
raisins

1- to 1 3/4-pound bread bowl

1. Heat the caramels and cream in a medium saucepan, over low heat. Stir gently but frequently for 3 minutes, or until the caramels are melted and the mixture is smooth. Remove from the heat.

2. Spread one-third of the caramel mixture on the bottom of the bread bowl. Top with half the apples, pecans, and raisins. Repeat the layers, finishing with a layer of caramel. Serve warm.

CHEFCHRIS**VRATTOS'S**
SOURDOUGH**BREAD**PUDDING

*John's brother Chris is an accomplished chef and former
owner of Northern California's popular Christo's restaurant.
He is also the creator of this outstanding bread pudding recipe.*

YIELD: **6 SERVINGS**

2 cups milk

1 cup heavy cream

3 eggs

2 egg yolks

1 tablespoon vanilla

$1/2$ teaspoon cinnamon

$3/4$ cup raisins

Bread from the
hollowed-out bowl,
cut into bite-sized cubes

1- to 1 $3/4$-pound bread bowl

1. Preheat the oven to 350°F.

2. Combine the milk and cream in a medium saucepan over low heat, and bring to a gentle simmer. Remove from the heat and let cool a bit.

3. Place the eggs, egg yolks, vanilla, and cinnamon in a medium bowl, and beat until smooth. Add the raisins.

4. Stirring gently, slowly add the cooled milk mixture to the egg mixture. Add the bread.

5. Pour the mixture into the bread bowl. Wrap the bowl with aluminum foil, leaving the top uncovered. Place the bowl on a baking sheet in the middle of the oven, and bake for 40 minutes or until the top browns. Carefully remove the foil and continue to bake another 3 minutes.

6. While the pudding bakes, prepare the sauce. Heat the brown sugar and rum in a small saucepan over low heat, while stirring to dissolve the sugar. Combine the cornstarch and water, then add it to the saucepan along with the cream. Increase the heat and bring to a gentle boil for 4 minutes, or until the sauce thickens. Remove from heat, and let cool.

7. Spoon portions of the bread pudding onto individual serving plates, drizzle with sauce, and serve.

SAUCE

2 cups brown sugar

1/2 cup rum (preferably dark)

1 teaspoon cornstarch

1 tablespoon cold water

1/2 cup heavy cream

AFTER-**DINNER** **VANILLA**PARFAIT

Chunks of sourdough are deliciously drunk with liqueur,
and then layered between creamy vanilla pudding
in this show-stopping parfait.

YIELD: 4 SERVINGS

½ cup dark rum

½ cup peppermint schnapps

½ cup amaretto

Bread from the
hollowed-out bowl,
cut into bite-sized cubes

3 cups vanilla pudding

Chopped fresh mint
for garnish

Chopped fresh rosemary
for garnish (optional)

1- to 1¾-pound bread bowl

1. Drizzle (do not soak) one-third of the bread cubes with rum, one-third with schnapps, and one-third with amaretto.

2. Layer one-fourth of the pudding on the bottom of the bread bowl, and top with the rum-flavored bread cubes. Add another layer of pudding, and top with the schnapps-flavored bread. Follow with another pudding layer, top with the amaretto-flavored cubes, and end with the remaining vanilla pudding

3. Garnish with mint and rosemary, if using, before serving.

12. Pumpernickel, Rye, and Other Bread Bowls

Sourdough is a clear winner when it comes to bread bowl cuisine. Its thick, sturdy crust and unobtrusive flavor makes it the perfect serving vessel for a variety of dishes. It is not, however, the only bread type that can house foods successfully. Readily available in most bakeries and supermarkets, rounds of hearty rye, pumpernickel, and whole wheat, as well as thick-crusted Italian bread are other great choices. (If you don't see what you're looking for, be sure to ask.) Although these breads make suitable bowls, typically, they are lighter than sourdough with crusts that are not as sturdy. For this reason, it is important to use them for dishes that contain minimal liquid.

From appetizers and entrées to salads and desserts, the choices on the following pages work well in various bread bowl types. The Carrot-Ginger Dip (compliments of Chef Peter Vroundgos) is perfect when housed in a wholesome whole wheat round, while the hot-and-hearty Apple-Sausage Stew and scrumptious Noodle Kugel find suitable residency in a dark and delicious pumpernickel bowl. A round of rye is the perfect serving vessel for our sandwiches like Sky-High Reuben and Gourmet Ham and Cheese. And Italian bread bowls are filled with flavorful Caesar Salad as well as savory servings of Spaghetti and Meatballs. Rounding out the chapter is a light and luscious Tropical Meringue Nest—served in a round of delectable Hawaiian sweet bread.

So get ready to add these outstanding recipes to your existing sourdough bread favorites. We hope they will inspire you to serve some of your own special dishes in different types of bread bowls. Have fun!

SPAGHETTI**AND**MEATBALLS IN**AN**ITALIAN**BREAD**BOWL

2 tablespoons olive oil

3 cups spaghetti sauce

8 ounces spaghetti

2 cloves garlic, halved

2 tablespoons butter, softened

½ cup freshly grated
Parmesan cheese

1- to 1¾-pound Italian
semolina bread bowl

MEATBALLS

8 ounces ground veal, pork,
or beef (or a combination of)

1 egg, beaten

1 clove garlic, minced

¼ cup breadcrumbs*

2 tablespoons freshly grated
Parmesan cheese

2 tablespoons freshly grated
Romano cheese

¼ teaspoon ground nutmeg

⅛ teaspoon salt

⅛ teaspoon black pepper

*To make breadcrumbs from the
hollowed-out bowl, see page 13.

*There's nothing like warm, crunchy garlic bread alongside a plate
of spaghetti and meatballs. In this recipe, a garlicky bread bowl
houses this popular entrée.*

1. Place all of the meatball ingredients in a large bowl, and mix with your hands until well-combined. Roll into mini meatballs the size of ping-pong balls.

2. Heat the oil in a large deep skillet over medium-low heat. Add the meatballs and brown on all sides. Using a deep spoon, remove any excess oil from the skillet, then add the sauce. Bring to a boil, then reduce the heat to low. Simmer for 20 minutes, stirring occasionally.

3. While the sauce simmers, cook the spaghetti al dente according to package directions. Do not overcook. Drain well, add to the sauce, and gently toss to coat well. Leave over very low heat until ready to serve.

4. Preheat the oven to 350°F.

5. Rub the cut sides of the garlic halves on the inside of the bread bowl, then coat with butter. Sprinkle with Parmesan, patting it onto the bottom and sides of the bowl.

6. Place in the oven and bake for 3 minutes, or until the bowl is hot and the cheese is melted. Remove from the oven, fill with spaghetti and meatballs, and serve.

CAESARSALAD IN AN ITALIAN BREAD BOWL

Housed in a bread bowl that has been flavored with
fresh garlic, anchovy paste, and grated Parmesan cheese,
this magnificent Caesar salad is truly fit for a king.

1. Rub the cut sides of the garlic halves on the inside of the bread bowl, then add a very light coat of anchovy paste. Drizzle with lemon juice and Parmesan cheese. Set aside.

2. To prepare the dressing, place the anchovy paste, garlic, lemon juice, mustard, Worcestershire sauce, and Tabasco sauce in a blender. Blend, while slowly adding the olive oil until the dressing is emulsified. Add the Parmesan cheese, salt, and pepper.

3. In a large bowl, toss the lettuce with the dressing. Spoon the salad into the bread bowl and serve.

YIELD: 4 SERVINGS

2 cloves garlic, halved

2 tablespoons anchovy paste

1 tablespoon lemon juice

1 tablespoon freshly grated Parmesan cheese

6 cups romaine lettuce, torn into bite-sized pieces

1- to 1 3/4-pound Italian semolina bread bowl

DRESSING

1 1/2 teaspoons anchovy paste

1 clove garlic, minced

1 tablespoon lemon juice

1 1/2 teaspoons Dijon mustard

1 1/2 teaspoons Worcestershire sauce

3 drops Tabasco sauce

1/2 cup olive oil

1 tablespoon freshly grated Parmesan cheese

Salt, to taste

Black pepper, to taste

CHEF**PETER**VROUNDGOS'S **CARROT**-GINGER**DIP** IN**A**WHOLE **WHEAT** BOWL

*Peter Vroundgos, John's cousin and owner
of Chef Peter V. Catering, uses fresh ginger
to give this luscious dip its Asian flair.*

YIELD: 8 SERVINGS

1 ½ teaspoons vegetable oil

½ medium onion,
coarsely chopped

1 pound carrots, peeled

1 cup vegetable broth

2 teaspoons sliced fresh ginger

2 packages (8 ounces each)
cream cheese, softened

½ cup sour cream

½ cup plain yogurt

½ teaspoon salt

¼ teaspoon black pepper

Chopped fresh dill for garnish

Bread from the hollowed-out
bowl for dipping

1- to 1¾-pound whole
wheat bread bowl

1. Heat the oil in a large heavy saucepan over medium-low heat. Add the onion and cook, stirring frequently, for 5 minutes or until soft but not brown. Continuing to stir, add the carrots and cook 3 minutes. Add the broth, increase the heat, and bring to a boil. Reduce the heat to low, and simmer 5 minutes or until the carrots are tender.

2. Carefully transfer the mixture to a blender or food processor, and purée until smooth, slowly adding the ginger. (You can do this in two or three batches.)

3. Transfer the puréed mixture to a large bowl along with the cream cheese, sour cream, and yogurt. Using an electric hand mixer or wooden spoon, beat until well blended. Stir in the salt and pepper.

4. Spoon the dip into the bread bowl and garnish with dill. Serve with chunks of whole wheat bread.

NOODLEKUGEL
INA**PUMPERNICKEL**BOWL

*A dark round of hearty German pumpernickel is the
perfect home for this noodle pudding. It makes a
memorable side dish or a light dessert.*

YIELD: 6 SERVINGS

2 ½ cups broad egg noodles

¾ cup brown sugar

2 tablespoons butter

I teaspoon vanilla extract

I cup boiling water

¾ cup all-purpose flour

I teaspoon baking powder

¼ cup granulated sugar

½ cup milk

½ cup raisins

½ cup chopped walnuts

2 ½ teaspoons ground
cinnamon

I- to I ¾-pound
pumpernickel bread bowl

1. Preheat the oven to 350°F. Grease a 9-inch baking pan and
set aside.

2. Cook the noodles according to package directions until al
dente. Do not overcook.

3. While the noodles cook, combine the brown sugar, butter,
vanilla, and boiling water in a small bowl. Set aside.

4. In a medium bowl, combine the flour, baking powder, and
granulated sugar. Add the milk and gently stir to form a
batter. Add the raisins and walnuts. Set aside.

5. Drain the cooked noodles and transfer to the baking pan.
Spoon the vanilla-brown sugar mixture over the noodles,
and top with rounded tablespoonfuls of batter. Bake for 35
minutes, or until the top is golden and the pudding is hot
and bubbly. Remove from the oven and let cool 5 minutes.

6. Sprinkle the interior of the bread bowl with cinnamon, then
place the bowl in the oven and warm for 5 minutes. Cut the
pudding into squares, transfer to the warm bread bowl, and
serve.

APPLE-SAUSAGE**STEW** IN**A**PUMPERNICKEL**BOWL**

A touch of sage accents the flavorful bratwurst, juicy apples, and
plump raisins in this hot and hearty stew. Delicious!

YIELD: 4 SERVINGS

2 cups apple cider

1/2 cup raisins

1 1/2 tablespoons butter

1 medium onion, diced

3 stalks celery, diced

1 1/2 pounds bratwurst

3 red delicious apples, peeled and diced

1 teaspoon finely chopped fresh sage

1/4 teaspoon salt

1/4 teaspoon black pepper

1- to 1 3/4-pound pumpernickel bread bowl

1. Preheat the oven to 350°F.

2. Bring the cider to a boil in a small saucepan over medium heat. Add the raisins and boil for 2 minutes. Remove from the stove and let the raisins steep in the liquid.

3. Melt the butter in a large deep skillet over medium-low heat. Add the onion and celery, and cook 5 minutes, or the onions are soft and translucent.

4. Cut the bratwurst into bite-sized chunks, add to the skillet, and brown on all sides. Add the apples, sage, salt, and pepper, and cook an additional 5 minutes, stirring frequently. Add the steeped raisins and half the cider. Increase the heat and bring to a boil. Reduce the heat to low, cover and simmer for 20 minutes. (Discard the remaining cider.)

5. Place the bread bowl in the oven and warm for 5 minutes. Ladle the stew into the warm bowl and serve.

GOURMETHAM**AND** CHEESE**ON**RYE

Layers of honey ham, Cheddar and pepperjack cheese,
and pimiento-stuffed olives are piled into a warm rye bread bowl,
and then cut into wedges and served. The classic ham
and cheese on rye never tasted so good!

YIELD: 4 SERVINGS

³/₄ cup pimento-stuffed green olives, rinsed well

¹/₄ cup Dijon mustard

2 tablespoons water

Bread from the hollowed out bowl, torn into bite-sized chunks

I cup port-wine-flavored soft Cheddar cheese

1 ¹/₂ pounds deli-style honey ham

8 ounces Monterey pepperjack cheese, cut into small chunks

I- to 1³/₄-pound rye bread bowl

1. Preheat the oven to 350°F. Dice the olives and set aside.

2. In a medium bowl, combine the mustard and water. Dip the bread chunks in the mixture to lightly coat (do not saturate). Set aside.

3. Spread a thin layer of Cheddar on the interior of the bread bowl. Cut the remaining cheese into small chunks.

4. Layer one-fourth of the ham in the bottom of the bowl. Top with one-fourth of the mustard-flavored bread chunks, Cheddar, pepperjack, and olives. Repeat the layers, ending with the olives.

5. Wrap the bowl with aluminum foil, leaving the top uncovered. Place the bowl on a baking sheet in the middle of the oven, and bake for 12 minutes or until heated through. Carefully remove the foil and continue to bake another 3 minutes.

6. When cool enough to handle, cut into wedges and serve.

SKY-HIGH**REUBEN**ON**RYE**

The Reuben sandwich is such simple perfection—
slices of hot corned beef on rye, topped with sauerkraut,
and covered by a blanket of melting Swiss cheese.
Add a little mustard, and you've got yourself a meal!

YIELD: 4 SERVINGS

2 ½ tablespoons mustard

I pound deli-style corned beef

I pound sliced Swiss cheese

I ½ cups sauerkraut

I- to I ¾-pound rye bread bowl

1. Preheat the oven to 350°F.

2. Using a spoon, spread the mustard on the inside of the bread bowl.

3. Layer one-fourth of the corned beef in the bottom of the bowl. Top with one-fourth of the Swiss cheese, and one-fourth of the sauerkraut. Repeat the layers, ending with the sauerkraut.

4. Wrap the bowl with aluminum foil, leaving the top uncovered. Place the bowl on a baking sheet in the middle of the oven, and bake for 12 minutes or until heated through. Carefully remove the foil and continue to bake another 3 minutes.

5. When cool enough to handle, cut into wedges and serve.

TROPICALMERINGUENESTINA HAWAIIANSWEETBREADBOWL

A bowl made from a round of Hawaiian sweet bread
is the perfect nest for this phenomenal dessert.

1. Preheat the oven to 350°F.

2. To prepare the meringue, place the egg whites, vanilla, and cream of tarter in an electric mixing bowl. Beat on low speed for 2 minutes, or until soft peaks form. Continue to beat, gradually adding the sugar a tablespoon at a time, until the peaks stiffen.

3. Using the back of a spoon, spread the meringue on the bottom and sides of the bread bowl. Place the bowl (still in its tin), on a baking sheet in the middle of the oven, and bake for 12 minutes or until the meringue is lightly browned. Remove from the oven and let cool a few minutes.

4. While the meringue bakes, cut the bananas into bite-sized slices and sprinkle with lemon juice to prevent them from turning brown.

5. When the meringue has cooled, add the bananas, pineapple, and papaya. Sprinkle with pineapple juice, macadamia nuts, and coconut. Top with scoops of vanilla ice cream and drizzle with warm caramel sauce. Serve immediately.

<u>YIELD:</u> **6 SERVINGS**

5 ripe bananas

1 teaspoon lemon juice

2 cups fresh pineapple chunks

1 cup papaya chunks

1/4 cup pineapple juice

1/2 cup chopped
macadamia nuts

1/4 cup shredded
sweetened coconut

1 pint vanilla ice cream

3/4 cup caramel sauce, warmed

1-pound Hawaiian or other
sweet bread bowl*

MERINGUE
3 egg whites

1/2 teaspoon vanilla extract

1/4 teaspoon cream of tartar

6 tablespoons sugar

---

* Hawaiian sweet bread is available in many major supermarkets. It often comes in a tin, which should not be removed when preparing this recipe. If the bread does not come in a tin, place it in an aluminum pie plate before preparing the recipe.

METRIC CONVERSION TABLES

COMMON LIQUID CONVERSIONS

Measurement	=	Milliliters
1/4 teaspoon	=	1.25 milliliters
1/2 teaspoon	=	2.50 milliliters
3/4 teaspoon	=	3.75 milliliters
1 teaspoon	=	5.00 milliliters
1 1/4 teaspoons	=	6.25 milliliters
1 1/2 teaspoons	=	7.50 milliliters
1 3/4 teaspoons	=	8.75 milliliters
2 teaspoons	=	10.0 milliliters
1 tablespoon	=	15.0 milliliters
2 tablespoons	=	30.0 milliliters

Measurement	=	Liters
1/4 cup	=	0.06 liters
1/2 cup	=	0.12 liters
3/4 cup	=	0.18 liters
1 cup	=	0.24 liters
1 1/4 cups	=	0.30 liters
1 1/2 cups	=	0.36 liters
2 cups	=	0.48 liters
2 1/2 cups	=	0.60 liters
3 cups	=	0.72 liters
3 1/2 cups	=	0.84 liters
4 cups	=	0.96 liters
4 1/2 cups	=	1.08 liters
5 cups	=	1.20 liters
5 1/2 cups	=	1.32 liters

CONVERTING FAHRENHEIT TO CELSIUS

Fahrenheit	=	Celsius
200–205	=	95
220–225	=	105
245–250	=	120
275	=	135
300–305	=	150
325–330	=	165
345–350	=	175
370–375	=	190
400–405	=	205
425–430	=	220
445–450	=	230
470–475	=	245
500	=	260

CONVERSION FORMULAS

LIQUID

When You Know	Multiply By	To Determine
teaspoons	5.0	milliliters
tablespoons	15.0	milliliters
fluid ounces	30.0	milliliters
cups	0.24	liters
pints	0.47	liters
quarts	0.95	liters

WEIGHT

When You Know	Multiply By	To Determine
ounces	28.0	grams
pounds	0.45	kilograms

Index

KITCHEN QUICKIES

Great, Satisfying Meals in Minutes

Marie Caratozzolo and Joanne Abrams

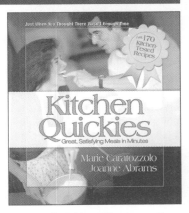

Ever feel that there aren't enough hours in the day to enjoy life's pleasures? Whether you're dealing with problems on the job, chasing after kids on the home front, or simply running from errand to errand, the evening probably finds you longing for a great meal, but without the time to prepare one.

Kitchen Quickies offers a solution. Virtually all of its over 170 kitchen-tested recipes call for a maximum of only five main ingredients, and each dish takes just minutes to prepare! Imagine whipping up dishes like Southwestern Tortilla Pizzas, Super Salmon Burgers, and Tuscan-Style Fusilli—in no time flat! As a bonus, these delicious dishes are good for you—low in fat and high in nutrients!

So the next time you think that there's simply no time to cook a great meal, pick up *Kitchen Quickies.* Who knows? You may even have time for a few "quickies" of your own.

$14.95 US / $22.50 CAN • 240 pages • 7.5 x 9-inch quality paperback • Full-color photos • Cooking • ISBN 0-7570-0085-1

MRS. CUBBISON'S BEST STUFFING COOKBOOK

Sensational Stuffings for Poultry, Meats, Fish, Side Dishes, and More

Edited by Leo Pearlstein and Lisa Messinger

When you think of stuffing, you probably picture Thanksgiving, turkey, and traditional dinner fare. But now that people all over the country are enjoying exciting new flavors, from fusion cooking to ethnic cuisine, maybe it's time to add a little pizzazz to your stuffing—and to your everyday meals, as well! Designed to take stuffing to new culinary heights, here is a superb collection of creative recipes from America's number-one stuffing expert, Mrs. Sophie Cubbison.

Mrs. Cubbison's Best Stuffing Cookbook is a complete guide to the art of making delicious stuffing. It begins with the basics of preparing stuffing, and then offers one hundred easy-to-make kitchen-tested recipes--from Jambalaya Stuffing to Asian Ginger Stir-Fried, and from Citrus Yam Stuffing to Onion Soufflé. Within its "Shaping Up" chapter, you'll learn how to turn stuffing into mouth-watering muffins, pick-up appetizers, and tempting desserts. Mrs. Cubbison has even included delicious low-fat, reduced-calorie recipes!

For over sixty years, pioneering chef Mrs. Cubbison reinvented the way we cook with stuffing. Today, her company lives on to reflect our ever-evolving tastes. With *Mrs. Cubbison's Best Stuffing Cookbook* in hand, you can add a touch of creativity not only to your holiday celebrations, but to every meal that you and your family enjoy.

$14.95 US / $22.50 CAN • 156 Pages • 7.5 x 7.5-inch quality paperback • Cooking/Stuffings • ISBN 0-7570-0260-9

THE MASON JAR COOKIE COOKBOOK
How to Create Mason Jar Cookie Mixes
Lonnette Parks

Nothing gladdens the heart like the tantalizing aroma of cookies baking in the oven. But for so many people, a busy lifestyle has made it impossible to find the time to bake at home—until now. Lonnette Parks, cookie baker extraordinaire, has not only developed fifty kitchen-tested recipes for delicious cookies, but has found a way for you to give the gift of home baking to everyone on your gift list.

For each mouth-watering cookie, the author provides the full recipe so that you can bake a variety of delights at home. In addition, she presents complete instructions for beautifully arranging the nonperishable ingredients in a Mason jar so that you can give the jar to a friend. By adding just a few common ingredients, your friend can then prepare fabulous home-baked cookies in a matter of minutes. Recipes include Best Ever Chocolate Chip Cookies, Blondies, and much, much more.

Whether you want to bake scrumptious cookies in your own kitchen or you'd like to give distinctive Mason jar cookie mixes to cookie-loving friends and family, *The Mason Jar Cookie Cookbook* is the perfect book.

$12.95 US / $21.00 CAN • 144 pages • 7.5 x 7.5-inch quality paperback • 2-Color • Cooking/Baking/Cookies • ISBN 0-7570-0046-0

THE MASON JAR SOUP-TO-NUTS COOKBOOK
How to Create Mason Jar Recipe Mixes
Lonnette Parks

In this follow-up to her best-selling book, *The Mason Jar Cookie Cookbook,* author and cook Lonnette Parks presents recipes for over fifty delicious soups, muffins, breads, cakes, pancakes, beverages, and more. And, just as in her previous book, the author tells you how to give the gift of home cooking to friends and family.

For each Mason jar creation, the author provides the full recipe so that you can cook and bake a variety of delights at home. In addition, she includes complete instructions for beautifully arranging the nonperishable ingredients in a Mason jar so that you can give the jar to a friend. Recipes include Golden Corn Bread, Double Chocolate Biscotti, Ginger Muffins, Apple Cinnamon Pancakes, Barley Rice Soup, Viennese Coffee, and much, much more.

$12.95 US / $21.00 CAN • 144 pages • 7.5 x 7.5-inch quality paperback • 2-Color • Cooking/ Crafts • ISBN 0-7570-0129-7